FOOTBALL SUPERSTARS

John Elway

FOOTBALL ⬤ SUPERSTARS

Tiki Barber

Tom Brady

John Elway

Brett Favre

Peyton Manning

Dan Marino

Donovan McNabb

Joe Montana

Walter Payton

Jerry Rice

Ben Roethlisberger

Barry Sanders

FOOTBALL ⬤ SUPERSTARS

John Elway

Samuel Willard Crompton

CHELSEA HOUSE
PUBLISHERS
An imprint of Infobase Publishing

JOHN ELWAY

Copyright © 2008 by Infobase Publishing

All rights reserved. No part of this book may be reproduced or utilized in any form or
by any means, electronic or mechanical, including photocopying, recording, or by any
information storage or retrieval systems, without permission in writing from the publisher.
For information, contact:

Chelsea House
An imprint of Infobase Publishing
132 West 31st Street
New York NY 10001

Library of Congress Cataloging-in-Publication Data
Crompton, Samuel Willard.
 John Elway / Samuel Willard Crompton.
    p. cm. — (Football superstars)
 Includes bibliographical references and index.
 ISBN 978-0-7910-9604-8 (hardcover)
 1. Elway, John, 1960—Juvenile literature. 2. Football players—United States—
Biography—Juvenile literature. 3. Quarterbacks (Football—United States—Biography—
Juvenile literature. I. Title. II. Series.

 GV939.E48C76 2008
 796.332092—dc22
 [B]
                        2007040951

Chelsea House books are available at special discounts when purchased in bulk quantities
for businesses, associations, institutions, or sales promotions. Please call our Special Sales
Department in New York at (212) 967-8800 or (800) 322-8755.

You can find Chelsea House on the World Wide Web at http://www.chelseahouse.com

Text design by Erik Lindstrom
Cover design by Ben Peterson

Printed in the United States of America

Bang EJB 10 9 8 7 6 5 4 3 2 1

This book is printed on acid-free paper.

All links and Web addresses were checked and verified to be correct at the time
of publication. Because of the dynamic nature of the Web, some addresses and links
may have changed since publication and may no longer be valid.

CONTENTS

The Play and the Lesson

The year 1982 was a difficult time to be a football fan. On September 20, members of the **National Football League (NFL)** Players Association decided to go on strike in support of obtaining more benefits, including higher minimum salaries, better medical insurance, and an improved pension plan. There would be no NFL games for 57 days.

Millions of fans, deprived of professional football, turned their attention to the college game. The day before the NFL season resumed on November 21, the most famous play in college football history would take place at the University of California's Memorial Stadium in Berkeley, California; one that muted the brilliant effort of Stanford's senior **quarterback**.

PLAYING FOR THE CARDINAL

Born in Washington State in 1960, John Elway had moved to southern California when he was a teenager. The most heavily recruited high school football player in the nation, he had chosen to attend Stanford University because of its long tradition of producing great quarterbacks, including Jim Plunkett, who was the first overall selection in the 1971 NFL draft.

From the moment he began to play at Stanford, in the autumn of 1979, Elway showed sensational ability with his arm: He could unleash rocketlike passes that had more velocity than most coaches had ever seen. But as great as his throwing arm was, Elway's legs were almost as important to his success, for he could **scramble** from the **pocket** and throw on the run better than almost any quarterback in the college game. Comparisons to NFL greats Johnny Unitas and Bobby Layne were common.

As great a talent as he was, Elway had not yet been able to lead Stanford to a postseason bowl game. In his freshman year, Stanford went 5–5–1; in his sophomore year, the team was 6–5–0; and in his junior year, the Cardinal had a dismal 4–7–0 record. None of this dimmed Elway's prospects; most experts believed he would be the number-one pick in the 1983 NFL draft, but, like most college seniors, he wanted his last collegiate year to be a memorable one.

Stanford began the 1982 season in fine fashion, defeating Purdue on the road, 35-14. But just one week later, Stanford was upset by San Jose State (which just happened to be coached by John Elway's father, Jack), 35-31. Stanford went on to beat Ohio State, 23-20, as Elway completed 35 of 63 passes for 407 **yards**, and to thrash Oregon State, 45-5, as Elway threw five **touchdown** passes. Stanford then lost to Arizona State, 21-17, in the final seconds of the game, and Southern Cal, 41-21, but came back to beat Washington State, 31-26. But the highlight of Stanford's season came on October 30 when it upended second-ranked Washington, 43-31. That victory brought attention from *Sports Illustrated* and seemed to confirm Elway's position

John Elway prepares to throw the ball during his senior season at Stanford. The two-time All-American completed 774 of 1,246 passes for 9,349 yards and 77 touchdowns during his four seasons as a starter for the Cardinal.

as the best passer in college football. At 5–3, it seemed as if Stanford was poised to finish the season strong and get to its first bowl game since the 1978 season. Unfortunately, Stanford then endured two painful defeats, losing to Arizona, 41-27, as the Wildcats scored 28 points in the last 12 minutes of the game, and to UCLA, 38-35. This meant that Stanford entered its annual "Big Game" against archrival California with a 5–5 record. The team's record was not inspiring, but the upset win over Washington and the win against an Ohio State team that would finish 9–3 meant that Stanford had a real chance of being invited to play in the Hall of Fame Bowl. To get there, the Cardinal had to beat the Golden Bears.

THE RIVALRY

Stanford University and the University of California, Berkeley (more commonly referred to as "Cal") had first played way back in 1892, when a young engineering student named Herbert Hoover (who later became the nation's thirty-first president) was the student manager for Stanford. Since 1902, West Coast observers had called the annual matchup the "Big Game," as heralded for them as Army-Navy or Harvard-Yale were for fans on the East Coast.

The Stanford Cardinal led the series, 40–34–10, but 40 of the games had been decided by seven points or less. Stanford had only scored 26 more total points than Cal in the 84 games of the series, and many a Big Game had been decided by a thrilling play or deception in the last two minutes. Fans from each school were convinced that theirs was just about the best rivalry going in the college game. As mentioned, Stanford came into the 1982 Big Game with hopes of being invited to a college bowl game, but Cal had no such hopes.

Cal had started the season by beating Colorado, 31-17, and thrashing San Diego State, 28-0. These victories were followed by a loss to Arizona State, 15-0; a win over Jack Elway's San Jose State team, 26-7; a humiliating 50-7 loss to then-top-ranked

Washington; and a 10-7 win against Oregon. By mid-October, the Bears were 4–2. They would then split their next four games—losing to eleventh-ranked UCLA, 47-31, and sixteenth-ranked Southern Cal, 42-0, and beating Oregon State, 28-14, and Washington State, 34-14—before the showdown with Stanford. Consequently, California's Golden Bears entered the Big Game with a 6–4 record, but the embarrassing losses to Washington and Southern Cal meant there was no opportunity for a postseason bowl game. About the best Cal could hope for was a victory over Stanford.

The rivalry between the two Bay Area universities carried beyond the football field: there was even an ongoing competition between the marching bands. The University of California, Berkeley was an iconoclastic school; the "Free Speech" Movement of the 1960s had been born there. But the University of California Marching Band is quite traditional: It was founded in 1891 and shares many characteristics of Big Ten Conference marching bands, including its high-step technique on the football field.

Conversely, the Leland Stanford Junior University Marching Band (hereafter referred to as LSJUMB)—which was named for Stanford's founder and former California governor and railroad magnate Leland Stanford—favors rock-and-roll songs of the 1960s and 1970s and performs in a more nontraditional style termed *scattering*, much to the displeasure of some of Stanford's more staid fans. The LSJUMB had chosen "All Right Now," a rock song by the British Group "Free," as the school's fight song.

NOVEMBER 20, 1982

In 1982, the weather was absolutely perfect for the Big Game: It was a clear, bright 57°F (14°C) day in central California. The two teams arrived at the stadium, went through their pregame rituals, then got down to the business of playing football.

The first quarter passed without a score. John Elway was contained by the Cal defense, and Stanford had to **punt** six times during its first seven possessions in the first half. Meanwhile, Cal scored 10 points in the second quarter, including a diving touchdown **reception** by **wide receiver** Mariet Ford in the **end zone**. The two teams entered halftime with California leading, 10-0.

Despite the deficit his team faced, John Elway was undaunted. He threw two touchdown passes in the third quarter, both of them caught by **running back** Vincent White. Stanford led, 14-10, until Cal kicker Joe Cooper booted a **field goal**. The Golden Bears still trailed by one point, but early in the fourth quarter, Cal quarterback Gale Gilbert threw a 32-yard touchdown pass to wide receiver Wes Howell, who made a one-handed grab to give the Golden Bears a 19-14 lead. California tried, but failed, on a two-point conversion attempt, and the score remained 19-14, with 11:24 left to play in the game.

This was a typical California-Stanford game, with everything coming down to the final minutes. Stanford kicker Mark Harmon nailed a field goal with 5:32 left in the game, making it 19-17 in Cal's favor. There seemed to be enough time for one final **drive**, but Elway **fumbled** on his own 33-yard line, and the Golden Bears recovered the ball with only 2:32 left. Remarkably, the Stanford defense held firm, Cal had to punt, and Stanford got the ball one more time, with just 1:27 remaining.

After a seven-yard loss on **first down**, Elway threw two straight incompletions, and the Cardinal offense faced a fourth-down-and-17 on its own 13-yard line with only 53 second left. Then Elway went to work. First, he hit wide receiver Emile Harry for 29 yards, then Mike Tolliver for 19 yards to get the ball down to the Cal 39-yard line. That play was followed by a surprise carry by halfback Mike Dotterer, who ran to the Cal 18-yard line. Dotterer was then stopped for no gain, but he was able to get the ball to the right hash mark, kicker Mark Harmon's favorite **position** on the field to attempt a kick. Harmon then booted yet another field goal, making it 20-19, in Stanford's favor, with four seconds remaining! Once again, Elway had rallied his team, and it appeared Stanford was bound for a bowl game. High above the stadium, Cal play-by-play man Joe Starkey told his listeners on WGO radio, "What a finish for John Elway, to pull this out. This is one of the great finishes. Only a miracle can save the Bears."

Certain that their team had won, the LSJUMB surged onto their end of the field. Horns blew, trombones sounded, and it seemed as if the Big Game was over, with Stanford engineering a remarkable fourth-quarter comeback. But there were still four seconds on the game clock.

Officials cleared the LSJUMB off the field and assessed Stanford a 15-yard penalty for unsportsmanlike conduct. Harmon had to place the ball on his own 25-yard line, instead of the 40. But that seemed to be a small detail. Thousands of Stanford fans were celebrating in preparation for a big victory; while thousands of disappointed California fans were starting to head to the exits.

Knowing there would be one last play, Cal **safety** Richard Rodgers told his teammates, "Look, if you're **tackled**, lateral the ball." Everyone just stared at him, so he repeated, "I mean, don't fall with the ball."

On the **kickoff**, Stanford's Harmon **squibbed** the ball, hoping one of the California players would simply fall on it. But by the oddest of chances, the ball went straight to Cal safety Kevin Moen, who had lined up five yards behind his usual position on the kick return team. (Had he lined up where he was supposed to be, the ball probably would have bounced over his head and the player behind him would have had to scramble to reach the ball before he would have been tackled.) Moen then fielded the ball at his own 44 and started running. But seeing a bunch of Stanford players approaching, he turned and threw backward, lateraling the ball to Rodgers.

Startled to get the ball, Rodgers began to run but found a Stanford **cornerback** right in his way. The play, and the game, would have been over if Cal **defensive back** Steve Dunn had not **blocked** Stanford cornerback Darrell Grissum, giving Rodgers just enough time to lateral the ball to Dwight Garner, back on the Cal 43.

"When Richard pitched it back to me, I made one fake and then attracted a crowd," Garner recounted later in Ron Fimrite's *Sports Illustrated* article "The Anatomy of a Miracle." About three Stanford players converged on Garner and it seemed he was down. Someone blew a whistle, suggesting the game was over, and several Stanford players and dozens of overeager Stanford fans, as well as members of the LSJUMB, surged onto the field.

Incredibly, Garner managed to lateral the ball back to Rodgers. This was the second time he had had possession of the ball, and Rodgers ran upfield from the Cal 48. He moved quickly, unsure which Stanford players were legally on the field and which ones had come from the **sideline**. Rodgers reached the Stanford 46-yard line, where, confronted by Stanford players, he lateraled the ball to Mariet Ford.

Ford got possession at the Stanford 47 and ran to the Stanford 27 where he was trapped by three Cardinal defenders. Rather than try to dodge them, Ford ran straight into them, creating a massive pileup, but he lateraled the ball behind at the last second, and it fell right into the hands of Kevin Moen, who had originally fielded the ball. What happened next was recounted in "The Anatomy of a Miracle":

> The Stanford band, 144 strong, was on the field by now. One bandsman, unaware that the game was being lost behind him, stood facing the Cal rooting section, waving his cap and dancing in victory. . . . Then, suddenly, Moen, in determined full flight, bore down upon them. Like a Red Sea, they parted for the miracle worker.

Moen ran into the end zone, tripping over and bringing down Stanford trombone player Gary Tyrrell (the two later

Cal safety Kevin Moen crosses the goal line and is about to run into Stanford marching band member Gary Tyrrell at the end of "The Play." With the touchdown, the Golden Bears captured an improbable 25-20 win over the Cardinal in what would become the most famous play in college football history.

became good friends *and* cultural icons in California football history). Incredibly, Moen had carried the ball twice, and Stanford had lateraled the ball a total of five times. Moen's touchdown gave California a 25-20 victory (there was no need to kick the **extra point**).

Joe Starkey had called many Stanford-California meetings over the years but nothing like this one. In the tense seconds and minutes that followed Moen's touchdown, Starkey spoke in quiet, hushed tones. Then, on learning the officials' verdict, he practically shouted:

The Bears have won. Oh my God, this is the most amazing, sensational, heartrending, exciting, thrilling finish in the history of college football. I've never seen any game like it in my life. . . . The Stanford band just lost their team that ballgame. . . . This place is like it's never been before. It's indescribable here. . . . I guarantee you, if you watch college football for the rest of your life, you'll never see one like this.

THE FALLOUT

While Cal fans went delirious with joy, Stanford fans went into shock. The entire Stanford team sat, fully dressed, in the locker room for 20 minutes. There were no recriminations; what had transpired was too wild and crazy for any one person to be blamed.

John Elway had completed 25 of 39 passes that day, for a total of 330 yards and two touchdowns. He had enjoyed a spectacular game on a personal level, but he had seen it all come apart in the last four seconds. Some fans placed the blame on Elway, for not letting the clock run down further before calling the time-out that preceded Mark Harmon's field goal, but this was like asking a man to prepare for a thousand-in-one chance. No one, not even the most optimistic Cal fan, had really thought that the Golden Bears would prevail in a game where they received a squib with four seconds to go!

Officials from the Hall of Fame Bowl left the game without issuing an invitation to Stanford. Despite setting a **National Collegiate Athletic Association (NCAA)** career record with 774 completions and a Pac-10 Conference record for yardage in a season (3,242), John Elway's career at Stanford would end in disappointment on that fateful day.

"These guys [the officials] ruined my last game as a college player," Elway said in the *Sports Illustrated* article. "This is a farce and a joke." What he meant is that Stanford players believed (and continue to believe today) that Dwight Garner's knee had hit the ground before he tossed the third lateral. If true, this meant that the play and the game should have ended right then. But the referees ruled that his knee had not touched, and that made all the difference.

Many observers agreed that it was a shame that a quarterback as talented as John Elway, who played one of the best games of his career, had to endure such a disappointing end to his career. But others felt it was a fitting end to just another in the long line of fantastic Stanford-California games, which had begun in the time of Herbert Hoover and continued to the present. The next day, as NFL players took the field for the first time in two months, the lead story on the popular CBS show *NFL Today* was of "The Play." Thousands of audio recordings of Joe Starkey's call of the game were sold; so were thousands of video tapes of the now-famous game. "The Play" became a celebrated part of college football lore.

And John Elway? He had been robbed, not by any one person—not even by the Stanford marching band—but by fate. He and Stanford deserved to win the Big Game of November 20, 1982, but they had lost it just the same. Elway was already known as a comeback kid in 1982, but he would take the lessons he learned on that disappointing day and harness them for the rest of his long career. To date, no NFL quarterback has amassed more fourth-quarter comebacks than Elway, who took his (painful) medicine in 1982 and applied it to an NFL career that lasted from 1983 until 1998.

Switch-Hitter

John Elway was born on June 28, 1960. He and his twin sister, Jana, both came into the world in Port Angeles, Washington, a small city on the north side of the Olympic Peninsula. Their parents were Jack and Jan Elway, who already had a two-year-old girl, Lee Ann. Although they did not know it at the time, their family would be complete with the arrival of the twins.

FATHER AND SON

Growing up, Jack Elway had been a talented football player with an enormous drive to succeed. His family had been known for its athletic prowess; Jack's father had been a high school football player, then a coach, and he had once played against the legendary Jim Thorpe. Big for his time (football players keep getting bigger with each decade), Jack was a standout at Washington State University until a knee injury in his sophomore year brought an end to his dream of achieving football stardom. Forced to find other ways to use his exceptional talent, Jack turned to coaching, and by the time his twin children were born, he was both the full-time coach at Port Angeles High School and a part-time coach for a nearby college.

By the time his son was three, Jack found that he and John were a natural match. Father and son delighted in playing all sorts of sports, with the son usually being the one who lasted longest: "God he was fun," Jack Elway later recalled in *John Elway: Armed and Dangerous.*

There were plenty of memorable moments in young John Elway's childhood, most of which revolved around sports. Jack and John played basketball against each other in the driveway. They played football in the backyard, and with the sun fading behind the horizon, little John would often ask for "one more" pass from his father.

Because of his own near miss when it came to achieving football greatness, Jack Elway was very conscious of how something could go wrong in a young person's life and career. He shielded his son in many ways, including keeping him off the ski slopes, where a bad injury could set one back for months, if not for years.

Meanwhile, Jack steadily moved up the coaching ladder. The family moved first to Aberdeen, Washington, where Jack became head coach at Grays Harbor College, and then to Missoula, Montana, where he became an assistant at the University of Montana. The elder Elway was making a name for himself as a coach, but it is safe to say his greatest source of satisfaction was a happy home, with two lovely daughters and one very athletically talented son.

The three Elway children were naturally competitive, both with each other and outside the home. John later remembered

John Elway gives the thumbs up to his father, Jack, after the Broncos defeated the Green Bay Packers, 31-24, in Super Bowl XXXII on January 25, 1998. Until the time of his death in 2001, Jack and John had a bond that was made even stronger by their mutual love of football.

that they would play the board game Risk for hours on end; consequently, their parents eventually banned them from playing the game in the house. The Elway children competed at Battleship and Monopoly as well, but when it came to outside sports, John was in a class of his own and could only be tended to by his father. "I never pushed John to play sports," Jack Elway later said in *Comeback Kid*. "He was always there waiting for me on the steps when I got home. I wanted him to have fun and be as good as he could be."

John showed his natural ability in a number of sports. He enjoyed playing baseball, football, and basketball, and he and his father played endless games of Ping-Pong in the family basement. Football did not become John's "special" sport until his early teens, but he was adept at throwing objects from an early age, as recounted in *Comeback Kid*:

> A bowling ball became an early favorite. We'd make a bowling alley in our hallway with plastic pins and balls. . . . Soon, I graduated from rolling to throwing. Sports balls, dirt clods, rocks, snowballs—you name it, I threw them.

Naturally this led to plenty of broken windows—both at home and at other people's houses—and young John had to do plenty of cleanup work and spend his allowance money on repairing windows. He had an exceptionally good relationship with his father, but occasionally he got into trouble, including the one time when Jack spanked his son for refusing to play ball with other children who had come to celebrate his birthday.

Throughout this period, the Elway home was tended to by Jan, who seemed quite happy with her role, though she later confessed she had driven to more games—home and away—and back from more late-night games than she cared to remember. Her "windshield" hours increased when John began to play organized football around the age of 11.

Fascinated by the Dallas Cowboys—especially by quarterback Roger Staubach and running back Calvin Hill—John joined the Evans Vance Company football team in Missoula, where they competed in "Little Grizzly Football." On the first day of tryouts, John went with the intention of asking to play quarterback, but he found he liked being a running back. When his father came late to the first game, John's coach said, "Either those players are the worst I've ever seen or your son is the best player I've ever seen." John had run for six touchdowns in that one game!

Jack Elway believed his son's greatest talent and potential was at quarterback, but he backed off from that stance and watched as John did just fine as a running back for his first two years in the game. After Jack spent some time as an assistant at his alma mater, Washington State, both father and son got a big break in 1976, when Jack was hired as head coach of Cal State Northridge.

The move from eastern Washington to southern California was a big one, and Jack Elway planned it well. Before deciding where to live, he scouted the area in detail, searching for a high school that would make the most of his son's athletic talents. Jack settled on Granada Hills High School, which, under Head Coach Jack Neumeier, had a tradition of throwing the ball, rather than running it. By then, 16-year-old John had shown he had a good arm—one that could evolve, with training, into a great one.

Elway started on the junior varsity team and soon began to throw more than any quarterback who came before him. From the beginning, he showed that he was willing to take chances, a quarterback who could, and would, throw the ball down the field. By the time he entered his senior year at Granada Hills, Elway was the most heavily recruited high school football player in the nation. But at the same time, he was also a basketball and baseball player, and quite good at both sports. It is safe to say that football was his most enduring love, but the young Elway loved sports, period.

He reached six foot two while in high school and gained another inch during his college years. His muscular body was the product of both of his parents, but, according to Jack Elway, John's height and all-round athleticism came from his mother. While still in high school, John showed superior mobility (a great ability to scramble from the pocket) and fantastic vision—he simply "saw" more of the football field and was able to complete passes to receivers that most quarterbacks could not.

Not all went smoothly, however. In the autumn of 1978, John injured his left knee. This was the type of injury Jack Elway had dreaded for so long, and it almost proved to live up to his fears. John had surgery in Los Angeles (he would undergo five knee surgeries over the years) and had to miss the rest of his senior football season. Despite the injury, Elway still completed 129 of 200 passes for 1,837 yards and 19 touchdowns during his senior season.

In the autumn of 1978 and the winter of 1979, John considered scholarship offers from a total of 60 different schools. Every major college and university wanted a player of his caliber, especially one who also did well in the classroom. Although many schools competed for him, Elway was able to narrow down his list simply by location: He wanted to play in sunny California. That ruled out many fine colleges in the East and Midwest, and reduced the list of suitors to a reasonable number.

Meanwhile, Jack again moved up in the coaching ranks, becoming head coach for San Jose State University in 1979. The elder Elway could have tried to influence his son's choice (it would have been wonderful, he thought, to have a father-son combination at San Jose State), but he left the matter to John, who ended up selecting Stanford University. The Stanford Cardinal had turned out many fine football players over the years, and its academic reputation was outstanding.

STANFORD

John Elway arrived at Stanford in the fall of 1979. Tall, lean, and blond, he exemplified the California-boy look of the 1950s, which was then undergoing a renaissance. Some Stanford students confessed they were prepared to dislike this outgoing but "square" freshman, with the sunny disposition, but most also admitted that it was hard to do. Trained by his father, Elway was consistently respectful toward his elders and friendly with his peers, and he refrained from letting alcohol, drugs, or bad behavior get in the way of becoming the best football player possible.

Majoring in economics, Elway proved a solid student. He was aware that it was a Stanford tradition that players miss practice rather than miss class, and he became a genuine scholar-athlete during his four years at the school. At the same time, he played both baseball and football for Stanford. Although his greatest ability was clearly in throwing a football, Elway also excelled as an outfielder and was a pretty good hitter; his father had taught him to hit left-handed as well as right-handed, from his earliest days.

During his sophomore year, Elway began dating Janet Buchan. A tall blonde, she was also originally from Washington State, and she was a champion swimmer on the Stanford team. The two became a popular couple around campus. There were some rough times during their early dates, however. Janet once broke a pinky finger while trying to catch one of Elway's throws.

Elway started for Stanford from the get-go. Under Head Coach Rod Dowhower, who would leave Stanford to take an assistant coaching job with the Denver Broncos after just one season, Elway helped lead the Cardinal to a respectable 5–5–1 record in the competitive Pac-10 Conference. Former Stanford player Paul Wiggin, who had been the defensive coordinator of the New Orleans Saints in 1978–1979, was named the Cardinal's new head coach in February 1980. He and John Elway scripted many plays together, but, as would also be the case when he was in the NFL, Elway had a habit of developing new ones on the fly. Many a college or professional coach might have become irritated by such a free-spirited quarterback, but Elway had a way of proving that he knew what he was doing. Time and again he scrambled, evaded a **sack**, and then threw for a big gain. Good coaches, such as Wiggin, know that long

During his time at Stanford, John Elway not only excelled on the gridiron but also played baseball for the Cardinal in his freshman and sophomore years. Then, when he was a junior, he was drafted by the New York Yankees and spent the summer of 1982 playing for their Class-A team in Oneonta, New York, where he hit .318 with a team-high 25 RBI in 42 games.

gainers can both create momentum and bring excitement to a team. Wiggin let Elway throw downfield whenever he could.

For John Elway, only one week out of the year was really difficult: the one in which Stanford played San Jose State. Jack and John were as close as a father and son could be; throughout his long career, John would claim that he owed everything to his father's tutelage. But the college game made no exceptions for fathers and sons—they had to play against each other, just like everyone else.

THE WEST COAST OFFENSE

Although he was very much a "West Coast" player, John Elway did not play in the **West Coast offense** at Stanford. Yes, the Cardinal offense threw the ball a lot with Elway at quarterback, but Coach Wiggin ran a pro-style offense. However, during the late 1960s and throughout the 1970s, a handful of West Coast coaches developed a new style of offense. At first glance it looked like any pro-style offense that threw the ball often, but what made it unique was that it used short passing plays to set up the run, rather than a traditional offense where the run was used to set up the pass.

Statistics became more refined and more important in the 1970s; coaches were able to determine the success or failure of any kind of play down to the smallest detail (the advent of personal video cameras helped, too). West Coast coaches, particularly Bill Walsh of the San Francisco 49ers, determined that, if the quarterback took quick three- or five-step drops and threw the ball quickly, while also implementing shorter pass patterns (within 15 yards of the **line of scrimmage**), the defense would have to commit to covering

Stanford and San Jose State met a total of four times—once a year—during John Elway's four college seasons. The Stanford Cardinal beat the San Jose State Trojans in 1979 (45-29) and 1980 (35-21) but was upset in 1981 (28-6) and 1982 (35-31). The 1981 game was especially painful for the Elway family as a whole. John was sacked six times by his father's defense, and Stanford gained less than a hundred yards on the day. When the game was over, father and son went to the nearby clubhouse where Jack Elway became noticeably upset. Hands shaking,

these shorter routes and would be vulnerable to both longer passes and the run. The West Coast offense, as run by Bill Walsh, took awhile to become established in the NFL, where most teams ran the typical pro set, with two wide receivers, a **fullback**, and a **tailback**, instead of up to five receivers and sometimes no running back. Although Walsh implemented the offense with the 49ers in the early 1980s, it did not become widespread in the NFL until the late 1980s and early 1990s, when coaches such as Green Bay's Mike Holmgren and Denver's Mike Shanahan, who both had ties to Walsh, began running the offense.

When Shanahan became head coach of the Broncos in 1995, he implemented a form of the West Coast offense for John Elway to run. So, despite playing in a run-oriented offense for the majority of his NFL career, Elway was able to throw the ball a bit more under Shanahan. Despite Elway's transition to the West Coast offense, traditional strong-armed quarterbacks such as Dan Marino and Jim Kelly remained linked to the earlier style of play.

he recounted in *John Elway: Armed and Dangerous* that, "As a father, I'm not very goddamned happy. John was obviously injured. He showed great courage." He felt that Coach Wiggin should have taken his son out of the game much earlier; only later did he learn that John had insisted on playing.

The pain of having to play against his father's team was a major roadblock in John's college career, as was the painful loss to Cal in the Big Game of 1982. However, John had accomplished much at Stanford. As mentioned, he set an NCAA career record for completions and established a new Pac-10 Conference record for passing. During his four-year career, he completed 774 of 1,246 passes for 9,349 yards and a school-record 77 touchdowns. He also set school records for touchdowns in a season (27) and a game (6). And despite Stanford's disappointing end to the 1982 season, Elway earned Pac-10 Player of the Year honors, was a consensus All-American, and was runner-up to Georgia running back Herschel Walker for that season's Heisman Trophy, which honors the top player in college football. As his college days neared their end, John Elway looked out and saw a world of opportunity.

THE YANKEES

Perhaps Jack Elway had told his son; perhaps John Elway figured it out for himself. In either case, John had to prepare for the fact

HEISMAN TROPHY VOTING—1982

	PLAYER	COLLEGE	CLASS	POSITION	NO. OF VOTES
1	Herschel Walker	Georgia	Junior	Running back	1,926
2	John Elway	Stanford	Senior	Quarterback	1,231
3	Eric Dickerson	SMU	Senior	Running back	465
4	Anthony Carter	Michigan	Senior	Wide receiver	142
5	Dave Rimington	Nebraska	Senior	Center	137

that he would surely be one of the first players selected in the 1983 NFL draft, which meant that he would most likely have to play for a team that had one of the worst records in professional football! In an attempt to introduce parity to the sport, NFL commissioner Pete Rozelle had decreed in 1971 that the team with the worst record the year before would receive the first pick in the draft. In 1983, that team was the Baltimore Colts.

To forestall this possibility of being selected by the Colts, Elway entered the 1981 Major League Baseball draft and was selected by the New York Yankees in the second round (52 overall). This was quite a surprise to those who knew only of his phenomenal football talents, but he had played baseball at Stanford during his first two years. In the summer of 1982, he accepted a $140,000 offer from New York owner George Steinbrenner to play for Oneonta, the Yankees' Class-A minor league team in upstate New York.

Elway got off to a slow start in the batter's box, but he played well in the outfield from the beginning. Long, lean, and downright fast, he chased down plenty of balls in the outfield. His hitting improved as the season progressed, and he ended up batting .318 with a team-high 25 RBI in 42 games. Steinbrenner praised Elway by saying, "I see a lot of Mickey Mantle in him," but others were not so sure. Many experts thought he might become a good baseball player, but he would never be as good on the diamond as he could be on the gridiron.

Elway refused to reveal which sport mattered more to him. He admitted he loved football, but he claimed he could see a real future for himself in baseball. However, many who were close to the family suspected that Elway and his father were using the possibility of playing baseball as leverage to scare off certain teams from drafting him.

THE 1983 NFL DRAFT

There had never been so many highly regarded players at one position in the history of the NFL draft. In the spring of 1983, there were six talented college quarterbacks available in the draft, any one of whom might be labeled a franchise quarterback. They were Todd Blackledge of Penn State, Tony Eason of the University of Illinois, Jim Kelly of the University of Miami, Dan Marino of the University of Pittsburgh, Ken O'Brien of the University of California, Davis, and, of course, John Elway of Stanford University.

Even given the number of outstanding quarterbacks available in the draft, there was little doubt that John Elway would be the number-one pick; he had shown sensational talent and the ability to deliver in clutch situations. But observers in the know believed that Dan Marino and Jim Kelly had as much natural talent as John Elway, and, as it would turn out, those two certainly were fortunate to be drafted later in the first round and thus not have to play for one of the worst teams in the NFL.

The Baltimore Colts finished with a 0–8–1 record in the strike-shortened 1982 season and, as a result, received the number-one pick in the 1983 draft for posting the worst mark in the NFL. The Colts certainly wanted Elway—that was a given—but he did not want them. Not only did Elway wish to play in warmer climes (such as California), but the hard-edged Baltimore coach, Frank Kush, was considered dangerous by John and Jack Elway. Robert Irsay, owner of the Colts, also stated his desire for the team to draft Elway. But Elway had an ace up his sleeve—his ability to play for the Yankees.

"I don't want to be a jerk or anything, but we [meaning Elway; his agent, Marvin Demoff; and his father, Jack] have been telling you for three months I'm not going to play in Baltimore," said Elway. When the Colts still tried to press the matter, Elway called a press conference and announced, "Right now, it looks like I'll be playing baseball with the Yankees. [The Colts] knew I held a straight flush and still they called me on it."

John Elway answers questions from the media during a news conference on April 26, 1983. Baltimore selected Elway as the number-one overall pick in the 1983 NFL draft, but he announced at the news conference that he would not play for the Colts but instead would play baseball for the New York Yankees.

That was it. Baltimore struck a deal with the Denver Broncos, which got Elway in return for **backup** quarterback Mark Herrmann; offensive lineman Chris Hinton, whom the Broncos selected in the first round of that year's draft; and a first-round pick in the 1984 draft. Elway signed a six-year, $12.7 million contract with the Broncos (this was the largest contract offered to an NFL rookie up to this point).

There was plenty of criticism for Elway. Football great Johnny Unitas, who had played for Baltimore, said Elway should grow up and pay his dues. Pittsburgh Steelers quarterback Terry

Bradshaw, who would retire after the 1983 season, said Elway had always been coddled by his family and that he could not make it in the real world. Coming from such legendary figures, these words had to hurt, but Elway had taken a chance and he was standing by his decision. He would be playing in Mile High Stadium in Denver, not Memorial Stadium in Baltimore.

The Mile
High City

After earning his degree in economics from Stanford in May 1983, John Elway headed to Denver later that summer. From almost his first day there, he was the toast of the town. Denver had always been a unique city. Located in the foothills of the Rocky Mountains, it was a distinctly "Western" city, but its social attitudes also looked east, to the American Midwest, which is where most of the original immigrants had come from. Residents of Denver were passionate about sports, especially football, and its citizens yearned for a team to match their desires, but until the late 1970s, the Broncos had been a disappointment.

ELWAY FEVER

It did not take long for Denver fans to adopt John Elway as one of their own. The Broncos franchise had been established in the summer of 1960 (the same year Elway was born), and Denver had been wild about its football team ever since. Unfortunately for much of the team's history, there had been little to cheer about.

Established as part of the new American Football League (AFL), the Broncos struggled during their early years, with

HOW THE NFL CAME TO BE

The National Football League is such an integral part of American culture today that football is considered the nation's most popular sport. But as sports historian Michael MacCambridge explains in his book *America's Game*, this was not always the case. Football had to earn its way into the American psyche.

Football has been played for nearly a century and a half, but the standardized rules of the game took a long time to develop. Baseball was "America's Game" from about 1920 (the decade when Babe Ruth and Lou Gehrig captured the nation's imagination while leading the New York Yankees to three World Series titles) until the late 1960s. MacCambridge argues that the turbulent emotional setting of the 1960s—a time when Americans were divided over civil rights issues and the Vietnam War—helped give football the edge over baseball, because football was more visual, dramatic, and intense.

Television played an enormous role in the sport's rise in popularity. As long as radio was the major medium by which Americans followed sports, baseball remained number one, but as television took over in the 1950s and 1960s, fans became more attracted by the drama that often unfolded during football games.

In 1960, a handful of businessmen created the short-lived American Football League (AFL) to compete with the already-

numerous turnovers in both management and coaching. In fact, during their first 13 seasons, they never had a winning record. And they were not able to make the playoffs until 1977, when they advanced all the way to the Super Bowl only to lose to the Dallas Cowboys, 27-10. In each of the next two seasons,

established NFL. The Denver Broncos played the first game in AFL history, defeating the Boston Patriots (they later became the New England Patriots), 13-10, on September 9, 1960. But having two leagues was bad for the game, and a merger was negotiated in 1966; although it was not finalized until 1970. The merger brought the AFL and NFL together as the new National Football League, which split into two conferences—the 10 AFL teams, along with former NFL teams the Pittsburgh Steelers, Cleveland Browns, and Baltimore Colts, would form the **American Football Conference (AFC)**, and the remaining 13 NFL teams would form the **National Football Conference (NFC)**. In 1970, the two conferences officially began to compete against each other, and Super Bowl V, between the Baltimore Colts and Dallas Cowboys, was the first true NFL championship.

The NFL has had its difficulties, especially in the 1980s, when there were two players' strikes, but the sport has been able to overcome many of its problems thanks to television. Not only is the Super Bowl the most-watched television event in the United States, but television rights to the NFL are the most lucrative of any entertainment property in the country. Consequently, television has become largely responsible for making football "America's Game," and Americans' love affair for the sport shows no sign of diminishing.

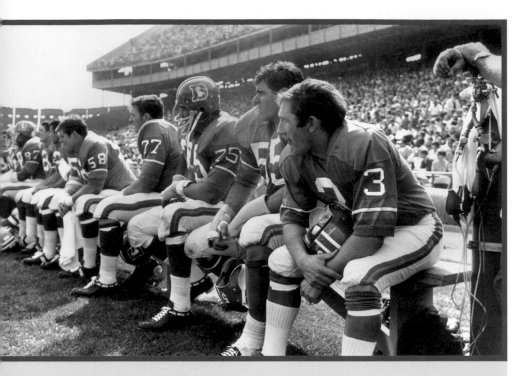

Denver Broncos players watch from the bench during a game with the San Diego Chargers in October 1968. That season, the team finished 5–9—one of 13 nonwinning seasons the franchise experienced until posting a 7–5–2 record in 1973.

the team finished 10–6 and advanced to the playoffs both times. In fact, the Broncos would not have a losing record until the 1982 season, the year before Elway was traded to Denver.

In 1981, Broncos owner Edgar Kaiser hired Dan Reeves, the 37-year-old offensive coordinator of the Dallas Cowboys, as Denver's new head coach. Born in Georgia, Reeves spoke with a distinctive southern drawl and was considered the model of a southern gentleman except on Sundays, when he could curse and rant with the best of them. Broncos fans knew that Reeves was an improvement, but they considered the arrival of John Elway in 1983 as an even more important piece to the puzzle.

Elway Fever took off in the summer and autumn of 1983, as no fewer than 50 reporters watched his every move. From them, Denver fans learned that Elway liked country and western music, that he was six foot three, and that he was an ardent fan of the soap opera *All My Children*. Hundreds of photographs were taken of Elway—in the locker room, on his motorbike, while he was running. By the time the 1983 season began, Elway had become the most popular celebrity in the history of the city.

ELWAY'S ROOKIE YEAR

Everyone knows that a professional athlete's rookie year can be tough, but few have had to deal with the kind of expectations heaped on John Elway's shoulders. Billed as the greatest quarterback to come out of college in a generation, he was expected to lead the Broncos to glory from the beginning. Making matters worse, Coach Dan Reeves had brought a highly sophisticated offensive system to Denver, with **formations** and terminology so complex that no one could be expected to learn everything in the first season.

Steve DeBerg had been Denver's quarterback in 1982, but Coach Reeves decided to start Elway in the Broncos' first game of the 1983 season at Pittsburgh on September 4. Needless to say, this provoked some animosity between fans and friends of DeBerg and those of Elway. (By a curious coincidence, Elway and DeBerg would be on different teams when they faced each other in one of the biggest games of Elway's career—see Chapter 8.)

Elway played well during the preseason, but in his first game as the starting quarterback, he stumbled against the Steelers. Throughout the game, Elway was harassed by the Pittsburgh defense: He was sacked four times, threw an **interception**, and completed just 1 of 8 passes for 14 yards. He was subsequently replaced by DeBerg after he bruised his elbow, and the Broncos eked out a 14-10 win.

From Pittsburgh it was on to Baltimore. Colts fans had neither forgotten that Elway had snubbed them that spring (when he insisted on being traded to Denver) or forgiven him for doing so. On one of the hottest Sundays on record, Elway stumbled his way through the first half before being replaced by DeBerg, who led the Broncos to a 17-10 win. In his first two games as a **starter**, Elway had completed just 10 of 29 passes for 120 yards. After his disappointing start, Elway had this to say in the locker room, as recounted in *John Elway: Armed and Dangerous*: "It hasn't been much fun so far. But I've gone up against Pittsburgh and the big buildup of my first game and Baltimore which loves me to death. Two of the toughest are out of the way."

If only that had been true. Elway's trials were about to continue.

During the next three weeks, Denver lost to the Philadelphia Eagles, 13-10; the Los Angeles Raiders, 22-7; and then the Chicago Bears, 31-14, before Elway was replaced as the starting quarterback. Elway was benched for the next four games, as DeBerg came in to rescue the Broncos' season. The veteran quarterback guided Denver to victories over the Houston Oilers, 26-14; Cincinnati Bengals, 24-17; San Diego Chargers, 14-6; and Kansas City Chiefs, 27-24. Elway returned to action in a 27-19 loss to the Seattle Seahawks on November 6, but he would not make a significant impact until the third-to-last week of the season, when he completed 16 of 24 passes for 284 yards and two touchdowns in a 27-6 win over the Cleveland Browns. Then, the following week against Baltimore, he had his best game of the season, completing 23 of 44 passes for 345 yards and three touchdowns. But overall, it was a disappointing season for Elway: He had managed only 123 completions out of 259 attempts, threw for just 1,663 yards, and tossed just 7 touchdowns against 14 interceptions. His quarterback rating of 54.9 was the lowest in the AFC, and the Broncos were eliminated in the **wild-card** round of the AFC playoffs by the Seattle Seahawks, 31-7.

For Elway, there were minor embarrassments to go along with the big ones. One Sunday of that rookie season, he went

A fresh-faced John Elway trots to the sidelines during a game with the Los Angeles Raiders in November 1983, his rookie season. Although Elway was expected to do well from the start, he passed for just 1,663 yards and 7 touchdowns, while throwing 14 interceptions, in a disappointing rookie campaign.

to call a play, and he lined up behind one of his **guards** instead of the team's **center**. Elway remembered in *Comeback Kid* that, "Everyone in the stands laughed at me. TV commentators asked: Is Elway a $5 million mistake?"

To make matters worse, Elway's rookie season in the NFL was measured against that of Dan Marino, his fellow "classmate" of 1983 who had been drafted by the Miami Dolphins. Marino had an outstanding year, completing 173 of 296 passes for 2,210 yards and 20 touchdowns, which made Elway look

MILE HIGH STADIUM

Originally it was called Bears Stadium, housing both a minor-league baseball team and the Denver Broncos, but a local civic group bought it and presented it to the city of Denver in 1968. During more than the next three decades, "Mile High" became nearly synonymous with exciting football games. The seating (and standing) capacity was expanded in the mid-1970s, and by the late 1980s, there were often 80,000 fans at Broncos games; a number that exceeded the amount of fans the franchise would get for an entire *season* in the mid-1960s.

Part of the excitement derived from the altitude of the stadium. Many football stadiums are at or near sea level: for example, Giants Stadium in northern New Jersey or the Superdome in New Orleans. But things were different in Denver, where the stadium is approximately one mile above sea level (5,280 feet or 1,609 meters), because the increased altitude plays tricks with the football, leading to longer punts, sharper spirals on quarterback throws, and easier field-goal attempts. Most fans agreed that the "thinner air"

and feel worse than ever. Elway did not face competition from Jim Kelly (another member of the "Class of 1983"), because Kelly decided to play for the Houston Gamblers of the short-lived United States Football League (USFL) before entering the NFL in 1986.

Given his dismal rookie performance, some members of the media believed Elway would cash in his chips and walk away from professional football. For example, Michael Knisley of *Sporting News* said:

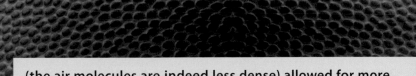

(the air molecules are indeed less dense) allowed for more dynamic football.

Quite a few teams had trouble adjusting to the dynamics at Mile High Stadium. The Kansas City Chiefs, perennial and hated rivals of the Broncos, lost many a game in Denver, and the Broncos were usually judged to have a strong home-field advantage, both because of the altitude and because of the fans. On October 1, 2000, Broncos fans even set a new world record for the loudest sustained cheer—for 10 seconds, the noise level reached nearly 129 decibels (which equates to the sound of a jumbo jet passing overhead), breaking the old record by more than 3 decibels.

Sadly, Mile High Stadium was demolished in 2002 to make way for the new INVESCO Field at Mile High. The run-of-the-mill Broncos fan (if indeed there is such a person) accepted the new stadium with grace, but diehards claimed the new stadium was nothing like the old one. Because he retired in 1999, John Elway was able to play his entire 16-year career in Mile High Stadium.

For this man, the Denver Broncos gave up Chris Hinton, Mark Herrmann and a No. 1 draft choice? For a man with a 47.5 **completion percentage**? For a man with twice as many interceptions as touchdown passes? For a man who was the lowest-rated quarterback in the American Football Conference? For John Elway? Where is the return on that investment?

He was, the media said, a talented college quarterback who had never faced real adversity until he had reached the NFL. Perhaps Elway did consider leaving the game. His rookie year had been a nightmare, and plenty of fans throughout the country started referring to him as a has-been. But Elway had always been a fighter. Whether at Granada Hills High School or at Stanford, he had been a gritty player who knew how to overcome difficult odds. He would come back for his second year.

MAKING PROGRESS

Elway decided to stay in California during the off-season. In March 1984, he married his girlfriend from Stanford, Janet Buchan. The couple then moved to Denver for Elway's second year in the NFL, which, they hoped, would be better than the first.

During the off-season, Steve DeBerg was traded to the Tampa Bay Buccaneers. Not only was Elway the new starting quarterback, but he also had a new position coach. After serving as offensive coordinator at the University of Florida, Mike Shanahan took over as Denver's quarterbacks coach in 1984. (He would then be promoted to offensive coordinator in 1986.) Although he and Elway had different personalities (the latter laidback and the former a bit more high-strung), they bonded quickly. Shanahan wanted to use Elway's offensive skills in a more dramatic fashion than did Dan Reeves—this difference of opinion led to many successes over the years but also to many conflicts among the three men.

In 1984, Elway and the Broncos started the season with a 20-17 victory over Cincinnati, but in the second game, the team was shut out by the Chicago Bears, 27-0. Then the Broncos caught fire. Although Elway's play was rather pedestrian, the Broncos defeated Cleveland, 24-14; Kansas City, 21-0; and Los Angeles, 16-13. The latter two were important victories because both the Chiefs and Raiders were AFC West Division rivals. Elway had his best performance in a Week 10 victory over the New England Patriots when he completed 26 of 40 passes for 315 yards and three touchdowns. More important, as a starter, Elway led the Broncos to a 12–2 regular-season record (13–3 overall) and their first AFC West Division title since 1978. He completed 214 of 380 passes for 2,598 yards and 18 touchdowns, but his performance was overshadowed by that of Dolphins quarterback Dan Marino who set NFL single-season records for completions, touchdowns, and overall yardage in just his second season. Denver made the postseason that year, but the team was upset at home in the divisional round of the AFC playoffs by the 9–7 Pittsburgh Steelers, 24-17. The game was tied with three minutes to play and Denver had the ball, but Elway was intercepted by Pittsburgh safety Eric Williams who ran it back to the Denver 2-yard line to set up the winning touchdown for the Steelers. Elway and the Broncos saw their postseason hopes disappear that cold December day. Everyone watching agreed, however, that Elway and the Broncos were getting better.

Elway came back for his third professional season in the autumn of 1985. By now he was a seasoned quarterback, with enough experience to call his own plays, but he was still being compared to Dan Marino. Conscious of this, Elway came into the season determined to prove his worth. He and the Broncos opened the season with a 20-16 loss to the Los Angeles Rams, but they came back to beat the New Orleans Saints, 34-23, and then easily defeated the Atlanta Falcons, 44-28. In these games, Elway passed for 873 yards and nine touchdowns. On

September 29, Elway had his first matchup with Dan Marino, a game in which the Dolphins' signal-caller outdueled his Broncos counterpart, passing for 390 yards and three touchdowns, as Miami edged Denver, 30-26.

Denver went on to beat Houston, 31-20; Indianapolis, 15-10; Seattle, 13-10; and Kansas City, 30-10. This contest was the beginning of what would become a long series of shoot-outs between the Broncos and the Chiefs. Both teams had rabid fans, and Kansas City's Arrowhead Stadium was every bit as difficult to play in for opposing teams as Mile High Stadium. After their 6–2 start, the Broncos went 5–3 down the stretch to finish the 1985 season with an 11–5 record. The Broncos became the first 11-win team since the AFL-NFL merger in 1970 not to earn a playoff bid, as the Los Angeles Raiders won the AFC West Division with a 12–4 record. Despite the disappointment of not making the playoffs, Elway set several franchise single-season records, including pass attempts (605), completions (327), passing yards (3,891), and total offense (4,414 yards). Elway and the Broncos would have to wait one more year for the glory that had been so long denied them.

THE DRIVE

In 1986, Elway and Denver started off red hot, beating Los Angeles, 38-36, to avenge two overtime losses they had suffered at the hands of the Raiders in 1985. Elway made his first appearance on Monday Night Football the following week in Pittsburgh, where he and the Broncos defeated the Steelers, 21-10. That was followed by a 33-7 rout of Philadelphia, a narrow 27-20 victory over New England, a 29-14 win against the Dallas Cowboys, and a 31-14 win at San Diego. The Broncos were 6–0, and running back Sammy Winder graced the cover of *Sports Illustrated*, which touted Denver as the hottest team in the NFL. Elway seemed to be putting his demons to rest as he threw for more yards than any other AFC quarterback up to that point in the season.

After the great start, the Broncos would split their final 10 games to finish the regular season 11–5 for the second year in a row. Fortunately this time around, their record was good enough to make the playoffs, as they won the AFC West Division and earned the second seed, behind Cleveland, in the conference.

In the divisional round of the playoffs, Denver beat the New England Patriots at Mile High Stadium, 22-17, on January 4, 1987, to earn their first playoff win since their 20 17 victory over the Oakland Raiders in the 1977 AFC Championship Game. With the win over the Patriots, the Broncos headed to Cleveland to play the Browns for the AFC Championship. On a cold, blustery day with temperatures in the 20s and a windchill factor in the single digits, Elway was matched against Bernie Kosar of the Cleveland Browns, a fine quarterback with about the same amount of experience as himself—though with not as strong of an arm.

Browns fans were known as the most rabid in the AFC. As if to emphasize the point, the team had designated a section of Cleveland Stadium near their own end zone as the "Dawg Pound," from which fans threw small dog biscuits at opposing players and teams. Elway and the Broncos knew they were in for a rough day on January 11: how rough, no one knew.

As the wind swirled and the fans howled, Elway and the Broncos quickly fell behind, 7-0, in the first quarter. Undaunted, Elway led the Broncos to 10 unanswered points to take a 10-7 lead in the second quarter, but right before halftime Browns kicker Mark Moseley tied the game. Broncos kicker Rich Karlis provided the only scoring in the third quarter, with a 26-yard field goal. The Browns then scored 10 straight points in the fourth quarter to take a 20-13 lead with 5:43 left in the game.

Then the Broncos found themselves behind the eight ball when kick returner Ken Bell misplayed the kickoff, which set Denver up at its own 2-yard line. Elway would have to lead the Broncos 98 yards to tie the game. In the **huddle**, held in its own end zone, the Broncos players took encouragement from the incredible words, "Now we've got them right where we want them!"

The immortal words do not belong to John Elway; they came from left guard Keith Bishop. But Bishop had spoken the truth. On first down, Elway threw to running back Sammy Winder for a five-yard gain. That was enough for some breathing room. The Broncos then called two consecutive running plays, as Winder ran for three yards and then two yards and a first down.

By now every player on the field had dirt on his uniform, but Elway was the dirtiest. The entire right side of his body was covered with remnants of the playing field, but he seemed to be reveling in the situation. After another three-yard run by Winder, Elway scrambled for an 11-yard gain for a first down at the Denver 26. Then Elway completed a 22-yard pass to running back Steve Sewell and a 12-yard pass to wide receiver Steve Watson to bring his team to the Cleveland 40-yard line at the two-minute warning. Elway had led the Broncos downfield, but the situation was about to take a turn for the worse. After throwing an **incomplete pass**, Elway was sacked for an eight-yard loss, which meant the Broncos faced a third-and-18 from the Cleveland 48-yard line. But Elway found receiver Mark Jackson for a 20-yard gain and a first down at the Cleveland 28-yard line. After another incompletion, Elway hit Sewell for 14 yards and a first down at the Cleveland 14-yard line with a little more than a minute left. On first down, Elway fired an incompletion but then ran for nine yards to set up the Broncos at the Cleveland 5-yard line. With just 31 seconds left in the game, Elway completed his sixth pass of the drive, hitting wide receiver Mark Jackson for a touchdown. After the extra point, the score was tied at 20-20.

In overtime, Cleveland won the coin toss and took the ball first. But the Denver defense stopped them, and Rich Karlis kicked the 33-yard game-winning field goal 5:48 into overtime

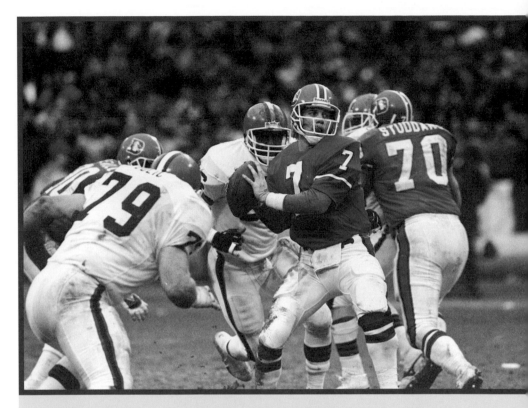

John Elway spots a receiver during the Broncos' AFC Championship contest with the Cleveland Browns on January 11, 1987. With 5:43 left in the game, Elway would lead the Broncos on a 15-play, 98-yard drive that would tie the game at 20-20. Denver would go on to win the game in overtime, 23-20, but "The Drive" solidified Elway's spot as one of the top quarterbacks in the league and was one of the defining moments of his NFL career.

to give the Broncos an improbable 23-20 victory—only the second conference championship game ever decided in overtime.

To say there was jubilation in Denver is to miss the mark. Broncos fans went wild with excitement. People started calling John Elway "The Duke" in honor of John Wayne. Before the game, Elway was just another strong-armed quarterback, but by leading a game-winning drive under such difficult circumstances, he had become one of the NFL's best quarterbacks.

He would later say: "That was my coming out party. It was my fourth year, but I hadn't really done anything great. That drive put me on the map."

Just as the last play of the 1982 Stanford-California game is known simply as "The Play," the sensational final Broncos possession during regulation of the 1986 AFC Championship Game is known simply as "The Drive."

Super Bowl
Setbacks

John Elway was "The Man" in January 1987. Not only had he pulled out a sensational victory over the Cleveland Browns, but he had rescued his own reputation, which had suffered in the three-and-a-half years since he first arrived in Denver. Now he was going to the Super Bowl, and everyone expected it would be the first of many appearances. As he headed off for the Rose Bowl in Pasadena, California, the site of Super Bowl XXI, Elway vowed to the Denver fans that the joy they had experienced in the big win against Cleveland would be surpassed by the joy they would feel when the Broncos were Super Bowl champions.

A GIANT CHALLENGE

The New York Giants had gone 14–2 during the 1986 regular season and had dominated the NFC. The team continued that domination in the playoffs, as they beat their two opponents, the Washington Redskins and the San Francisco 49ers, by a combined score of 66-3! They had an excellent running game, led by Joe Morris, who rushed for more than 1,500 yards, and one of the best coaches in the league, Bill Parcels. Although their passing game was not on the same level as that of the Broncos, the Giants were led by steady quarterback Phil Simms, who had thrown for nearly 3,500 yards that season. Most experts who analyzed the game thought that the Giants would have the edge in the running game, but the Broncos would have the advantage in the passing game.

There was plenty of buildup and hype before the Super Bowl. Elway and Simms both posed for dozens, if not hundreds, of photos, and there was talk of which quarterback would receive the most offers to endorse products after the game. But all this was just a prelude to the magic moments that commenced during the afternoon of January 25, 1987.

The Giants were heavy favorites but that was because of their formidable defense, not because of the Elway-Simms matchup. Elway came out throwing in the first quarter. Highlighted by a 24-yard completion to wide receiver Mark Jackson on third-and-seven from his own 37, Elway led the Broncos down the field to set up kicker Rich Karlis, who booted a 48-yard field goal. Karlis's kick matched a Super Bowl record and gave the Broncos an early 3-0 lead.

The Giants responded with a nine-play, 78-yard touchdown drive that ended with Simms throwing a six-yard strike to **tight end** Zeke Mowatt. Elway quickly answered the Giants' score by completing three straight passes for 36 yards. Then, after two 15-yard penalties by the Giants, Elway scored a touchdown from four yards out to give the Broncos a 10-7 lead. This Super Bowl was living up to its name, as the lead had already changed hands twice.

Simms and the Giants performed well in the second quarter but so did Elway. Denver held its narrow 10-7 lead for most of the quarter, but the Broncos suffered a disappointing setback after they failed to score when they had the ball first-and-goal at the Giants' 1-yard line. On first down, Elway was sacked for a two-yard loss. On second down, fullback Gerald Willhite was stuffed for no gain. Then, on third down, Sammy Winder was tackled for a four-yard loss. The Broncos at least hoped to salvage the drive with a field goal, but Karlis could not connect on a 23-yard attempt, which was the shortest field goal miss in Super Bowl history.

The Broncos were eager to head into the locker room to regroup, but Giants **defensive end** George Martin sacked Elway in the end zone for a safety with 2:46 left in the half to cut the Broncos' lead to 10-9. Amazingly, the Broncos again shot themselves in the foot right before halftime. After driving to the Giants' 20-yard line, Elway threw three consecutive incomplete passes and Karlis again missed a field goal, this time from 34 yards. Casual observers pointed to the fact that Denver still held the lead, but astute fans pointed to the Broncos' missed opportunities.

When the teams came out for the second half, few people guessed what was coming: the single best performance by a quarterback in the Super Bowl. And it was not from John Elway. Phil Simms was considered a solid quarterback, but since the Giants selected him in the 1979 NFL draft, he had been injured for the majority of his career. He finally righted the ship during the 1984 season, when he threw for more than 4,000 yards, earning him a trip to his first Pro Bowl. His recent accomplishments notwithstanding, Simms's performance in the second half of Super Bowl XXI was one for the ages. During one stretch of the second half, Simms completed 10 passes in a row. All told, he completed 22 of his 25 passes, which included two throws that were dropped by New York receivers.

The Giants took the lead on a 63-yard drive, capped by a 13-yard touchdown pass by Simms to tight end Mark Bavaro. This was the beginning of 24 unanswered points by the

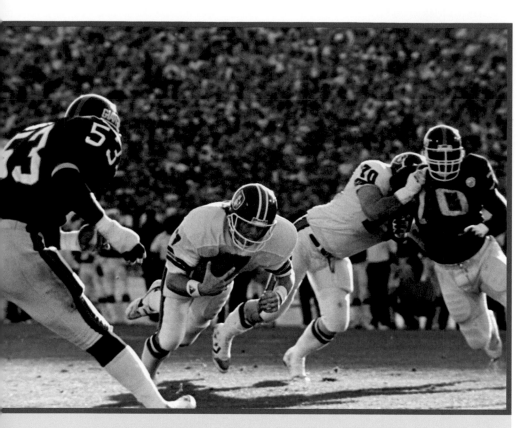

John Elway dives between New York Giants linebacker Carl Banks (left) and defensive lineman Leonard Marshall during the first quarter of Super Bowl XXI, on January 25, 1987. Although Elway scored on the play to give the Broncos a 10-7 lead, the Giants would score on their first five possessions of the second half en route to a 39-20 win.

Giants; all told, they would score four touchdowns and a field goal on their first five second-half possessions. Perhaps the Denver defense had worn itself out in the first half; perhaps the players were simply stunned by the avalanche of passes that came their way. The end result was a 39-20 loss, meaning that Denver only managed 10 points in the second half. In the win, Simms set Super Bowl records for consecutive completions, completion percentage (88 percent), and **passer rating** (150.9).

Although he cautioned fans not to get too excited by the win, *Sports Illustrated*'s Paul Zimmerman hailed Phil Simms and the Giants for their outstanding performance:

> The Giants are a young team. Only 7 players on the 45-man roster have reached their 30th birthday. If you're thinking dynasty, though, remember that the [Chicago] Bears were a young team when they won the Super Bowl last year. Strange things can happen to a club during a season. But right now the Giants are on top for the first time since 1956. They have made all the stops—dismay and hope and glory . . . you name it, they have been there. And so has Phil Simms.

The same could have been said of John Elway and the Broncos, who had come oh so close and had to go home empty-handed.

A NEW SEASON

Elway and the Broncos were disappointed by the Super Bowl defeat, but it seemed they had plenty of time to make up for it. Elway turned 27 the summer after the loss, and many of the key players on the team were around his age. His arm strength showed no signs of declining, so it seemed likely that he and the Broncos would return to the Super Bowl in short order.

The 1987 season was a new beginning for the Broncos. Meanwhile, *Sports Illustrated* proved uncannily accurate about the New York Giants and their hopes of becoming a dynasty; just one year after winning the Super Bowl with a 17–2 overall record, the Giants stumbled to 6–9 during another strike-shortened year. On the other hand, the Broncos started out strong and never looked back. They had three Monday Night Football appearances in 1987, beating the Los Angeles Raiders, 30-14; losing to the Minnesota Vikings, 34-27; and beating the

Chicago Bears, 31-29, another team that had been expected to become a dynasty after their amazing Super Bowl run in 1985. There were disappointing loses to the Buffalo Bills, 21-14, and the Seattle Seahawks, 28-21, but the main story of the 1987 season was another players' strike.

Although the season was only one game shorter than normal, replacement players, or scabs, as they were called by the NFL players, filled in for the striking players. They took the field for the Broncos in games three, four, and five and went 2–1 in those three contests. The Broncos lost their first game after the strike, the Monday Night contest with the Vikings, but rebounded to win their division with a 10–4–1 record (the tie was with Green Bay). Despite the shortened season, Elway was named MVP of the league by the Associated Press after he threw for 3,198 yards and 19 touchdowns. In the divisional round of the playoffs, the Broncos thrashed the Houston Oilers, 34-10, behind 259 yards passing and two touchdowns from Elway. The win set up a rematch with the Cleveland Browns in the AFC Championship Game.

Led by two Elway touchdown passes, the Broncos took a 21-3 lead into halftime against the Browns. But Cleveland fought back in the third and fourth quarters. The game became a shoot-out in the second half, as Browns quarterback Bernie Kosar threw three touchdown passes and Cleveland tied the game at 31-31 with a little less than six minutes left in the game. Elway then went to work. From his own 25-yard line, he directed a five-play, 75-yard drive that culminated in a 23-yard touchdown pass to Sammy Winder. But the Browns refused to give up. Kosar drove them all the way to the Denver 8-yard line with a little more than a minute left. He then handed the ball off to running back Ernest Byner, who appeared to have a clear path to the end zone. Fortunately for the Broncos, cornerback Jeremiah Castille stripped Byner of the ball and Denver recovered the fumble. Broncos fans were overjoyed to see their beloved orange- and blue-clad players in the Super Bowl for the second straight year. There they would meet the NFC champion Washington Redskins.

SUPER BOWL XXII

San Diego's Jack Murphy Stadium was the sight of Super Bowl XXII, which took place on a balmy January evening. Given the improvement the Broncos had made since their disappointing loss to the Giants, many prognosticators were betting on Denver. Elway seemed to have justified his position as one of the highest-paid quarterbacks in the sport; he had come a long way from that early, painful rookie season of 1983.

Lined up against Elway was Doug Williams, the first African-American quarterback ever to start in a Super Bowl. Thankfully for Elway, much of the attention (and pressure) was focused on Williams, as reporters badgered him at every turn. How did he feel that day? What did he think about being the first black quarterback to start in the biggest sporting event in the world? Most observers believed that Williams fielded the questions with class and alacrity—sadly, the same could not be said for the game's biggest handicapper.

The Broncos won the Super Bowl coin toss and chose to take the first possession. On the very first play from scrimmage, Elway lined up in **shotgun formation** (a tactic pioneered by the Dallas Cowboys in the 1970s). After receiving the **snap**, he had time to survey the field and see that Washington's defenders were spread out. Suddenly Elway lifted a magnificent 56-yard bomb that went straight to receiver Ricky Nattiel. Seconds later, after the extra-point attempt, Denver had jumped out to a 7-0 lead!

Broncos fans were constantly on their feet during that first quarter. Just minutes after his terrific touchdown pass, Elway actually caught a pass himself—the first quarterback ever to do so in a Super Bowl game. After handing the ball off to Steve Sewell, Elway went downfield and caught a 23-yard pass from the Broncos' running back, which led to a 24-yard Rich Karlis field goal that put Denver ahead, 10-0.

JIMMY "THE GREEK" SNYDER

Think tennis and Bud Collins comes to mind. Think boxing (especially in the days of Muhammad Ali) and one thinks of Howard Cosell. Similarly, one man was largely identified with professional football prognostication in the late 1970s and most of the 1980s. Jimmy the Greek was the man.

Born in Steubenville, Ohio, in 1919, Dimetrios Georgios Synodinos worked for local bookies at the age of 14 and kept moving up the ranks of sports betting. Moving to New York City, he kept making money—and acquiring fame—until he was investigated by the U.S. Justice Department. He then moved to Las Vegas, where gambling was legal, and became the best-known, if not the most accurate, of all sports forecasters.

In 1976, Snyder joined the *NFL Today* on CBS, where he discussed football with Brent Musburger, Irv Cross, and Phyllis George before leading the viewer into his "The Greek's Board" segment, where he forecasted who would win and lose that Sunday's NFL games. Thanks to the show's popularity, Jimmy the Greek became a household name, someone whom millions of small-time betters relied upon for sage advice (sometimes to their peril).

In January 1988, Snyder replied in an offhand way to a reporter who asked him a question about Doug Williams becoming the first black quarterback to start in a Super Bowl. Snyder let loose: "[The black] is bred to be the better athlete because he's been bred to be that way . . . the slave owner would breed his big black to his big woman so that he could have a big black kid." Although Snyder claimed he was speaking off the record, CBS promptly fired him. He died of a heart attack in 1996 and was buried in his hometown.

The momentum seemed to be with the Broncos, especially after they knocked Williams out of the game with a hyperflexed left knee a few minutes later. It was around this time that many Redskins players changed from half-inch to full-inch cleats to handle the soggy field. (Many of the Broncos' players had made the switch much earlier.) Perhaps the new cleats contributed to the single greatest quarter of offensive production in Super Bowl history, or perhaps it was because Williams returned to the game after missing a series.

In quick succession, Williams connected with wide receiver Ricky Sanders for 80 yards and a touchdown; then he connected on a 27-yard scoring strike with receiver Gary Clark. The Redskins were now up, 14-10, but they were far from finished. Running back Timmy Smith galloped 58 yards for another seven points, and then Williams again found Sanders, this time for a 50-yard touchdown pass. Finally, Williams completed an 8-yard touchdown throw to tight end Clint Didier, and the rout was on. Five touchdowns and 35 points in less than 15 minutes of play! The score stood at 35-10, and the game was only halfway over.

No matter how much berating went on in the locker room by the Broncos' coaches, everyone knew that John Elway could not make up this 25-point deficit. After all, the air had gone out of the Broncos' offense, as well as their defense. The Redskins added seven more points in the fourth quarter, bringing the humiliating final score to 42-10.

Few had criticized John Elway after the Super Bowl loss to the New York Giants, but he took plenty of heat after the loss to the Redskins. "John didn't scream at anyone in the huddle," said receiver Mark Jackson in *Sports Illustrated*. "He plays better when he's screaming at people. Usually, if you screw up, he'll tell you. For some reason, he didn't go crazy. John was too controlled today."

Elway appeared fatalistic in the postgame press conference. Asked if he had ever endured a worse loss, he mentioned the

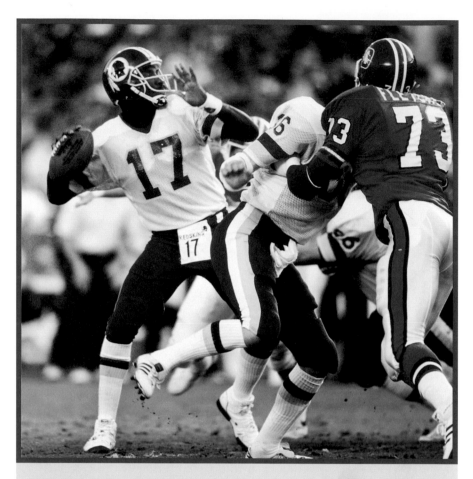

Redskins quarterback Doug Williams prepares to throw the ball during Washington's 42-10 win over Denver in Super XXII on January 31, 1988. Williams, who became the first African American to play quarterback in the Super Bowl, completed 18 of 29 passes for a record 340 yards and four touchdowns in the win.

Super Bowl defeat of the previous season to the Giants. Asked where the momentum of the game had changed, he simply said, "The second quarter." Asked if he felt he would never be viewed as a great quarterback unless he won the Super Bowl someday, he replied softly: "That's on my mind."

What could he say? The day, the game, and the Super Bowl ring belonged to Doug Williams.

Third Time Is Not the Charm

Every great athlete wants to win but also knows what it is like to lose. One could even argue that losing can help an athlete, by making him or her hungrier for the next opportunity. In the spring and summer of 1988, John Elway readied himself for another run at the Super Bowl. He had been in the NFL only five seasons but was already on the way toward achieving legendary status for his passing ability. But he had lost the "Big One" twice in a row and the sting of those losses remained with him for a long time.

THE NEW YEAR

Most Americans mark the first of January as the start of the New Year. Football players, however, see early September, or the first day of the regular season, as the start of their annual run for greatness. No one doubted Elway's determination to avenge the two Super Bowl defeats, but some commentators questioned his grittiness when it came down to making the big play in the big game. This seemed odd, given that Elway already had a reputation for leading comebacks in regular-season and playoff games; but he certainly had not been able to do so on the game's biggest stage. Unfortunately, the 1988 season would not give him an opportunity to show his best stuff.

The Broncos had acquired future Hall of Fame running back Tony Dorsett from the Dallas Cowboys in June, but he was long past his prime, and this would be his last season. In addition, Elway nursed knee and shoulder injuries throughout the 1988 season and the results showed on the field.

Denver started the season by losing to the Seattle Seahawks, 21-14, then defeating the San Diego Chargers, 34-3. They then lost two in a row, including a Monday Night Football meltdown in which they held a 24-0 halftime lead against their AFC West Division foe the Los Angeles Raiders but ended up losing in overtime, 30-27. After the tough start, they rebounded to claim three victories in a row, but just when it appeared the Broncos were back on track, they surrendered 94 points in two losses, including an embarrassing 55-23 rout at the hands of the Indianapolis Colts on Monday Night Football. Standing at 4–5 after the loss to the Colts, the Broncos still had a chance to make the playoffs if they played well down the stretch. However, the team remained inconsistent: One week, they would play lights out, as they did in a 30-7 win over the Cleveland Browns in Week 11; then the following week they would lay an egg, as they did in a 42-0 loss to the New Orleans Saints, which was one of the worst defeats in franchise history. Denver finished the season with a disappointing 8–8 record. After two straight AFC titles, the Broncos would be watching the playoffs from home this season. Elway threw for 3,309 yards on the season, but he also had more interceptions (19) than touchdown passes (17) and only managed one 300-yard game in the injury-plagued season.

AN AMAZING AUTUMN

The fall of 1989 was one of the most interesting and surprising times in recent memory. In November, thousands of East Germans broke through the Berlin Wall, which had divided East and West Germany for a generation. Thousands of young Eastern Europeans, weary of oppression, toppled Communist dictatorships throughout Eastern Europe. By New Year's Day, 1990, the configuration of Eastern Europe had changed. Democracy seemed to be spreading throughout the region.

Meanwhile, in the United States, San Francisco was rocked by a powerful earthquake on October 17, 1989. The quake hit just as thousands of fans were settling into their seats to watch Game 3 of the World Series, played between the San Francisco Giants and the Oakland Athletics. Needless to say, Game 3 was postponed, for a week, and both the sports world and the attention of the nation's citizens were focused on matters of relief rather than sports. But when the World Series resumed, and when the NFL resumed play that Sunday, it was apparent that the Bay Area quake had not harmed the teams from that part of California. The San Franciso 49ers won the first game they played after the quake, and they seemed like a good candidate to make a run for the Super Bowl that year.

Denver started its season well, too, beating Kansas City, 34-20, and defeating Buffalo in a Monday Night Football game, 28-14. In the win over the Bills, Elway recorded the longest run of his career, a 31-yard scramble that revealed how dangerous he could be when he left the pocket. A 31-21 victory against the Los Angeles Raiders followed, and even a 16-13 loss to Cleveland did not stop the momentum. Denver went on to beat the San Diego Chargers, 16-10, in another patented Elway fourth-quarter comeback; the Indianapolis Colts, 14-3; the Seattle Seahawks, 24-21, in Elway's best game of the season, as he threw for 344 yards; the Pittsburgh Steelers, 34-7; and Kansas City, 16-13. Although the Broncos fell, 28-24, to the Philadelphia Eagles after their win over Seattle, they were

John Elway drills a pass over the middle during the Broncos' 34-7 win against the Pittsburgh Steelers on November 5, 1989. That season, Denver won its third AFC West Division title in four seasons, as Elway passed for more than 3,000 yards for the fifth time in his young career.

in the midst of an 8–2 spurt that solidified them as a playoff contender. The Broncos then beat the Washington Redskins, 14-10, on Monday Night Football, despite the fact that Elway missed the game due to a bad batch of chipped beef he had eaten at the White House that morning. Although they only won two out of their last five games, the Broncos finished 11–5, won the AFC West Division, and earned home-field advantage throughout the playoffs.

The confidence of Denver fans grew as the season progressed, but they were unaware that Elway had been feuding with Coach Reeves throughout the season. The two men had never been totally comfortable with each other, but the tension began to mount that season, with Elway being frustrated by Reeves's desire to focus more on the running game than the passing game. Both men let off steam by airing their grievances to reporters, and the team was jittery, even fragile, as it headed into the playoffs.

THE POSTSEASON

To open the postseason, the Broncos hosted the Pittsburgh Steelers in the divisional round of the playoffs. Although they were no longer the powerhouse team they had been in the mid- and late 1970s, the Steelers still had tradition on their side, something the Broncos were building toward. The game seesawed back and forth, but Elway provided some last-minute magic in the fourth quarter, leading the Broncos on a 71-yard game-winning drive to give his team a 24-23 victory. Although he would lead the Steelers for two more seasons, Chuck Noll had coached his last postseason game. The future NFL Hall of Fame coach, who had helped orchestrate four Super Bowl wins, would retire after the 1991 season.

With the win by the Broncos, they advanced to the AFC Championship Game for the third time in four years. And, once again, they would face the Cleveland Browns. Entering the game, Elway was 5–1 in his career against the Browns, including the two AFC Championship Game wins. However, Elway's lone loss had come during the 1989 season, in a game in which he had only completed 6 of 19 passes for 198 yards. Although the Browns may have gained confidence from that win, Elway was a different player this day, as he completed 20 of 36 passes for a season-high 385 yards and three touchdowns in a 37-21 victory.

SUPER BOWL XXIV

This time the Super Bowl would pit the Denver Broncos against the San Francisco 49ers, considered by many experts to be the best team in football that season. Joe Montana, who had entered the NFL a few years earlier than Elway, was thought to be the best quarterback of his time, and commentators called it a match between the puncher (Elway) and the boxer (Montana).

However, for Elway, questions again arose about his ability to lead his team to a Super Bowl victory. One of the most aggravating moments came just days before the Super Bowl. Former Pittsburgh quarterback Terry Bradshaw, who was making himself into a ubiquitous presence in television advertisements and commentating, was asked if John Elway was a great quarterback.

"Nope," Bradshaw replied. "A good one." He went on to say that Elway had never developed beyond a certain level; that he had been babied by the Denver press corps and his coaches. Although Bradshaw did not explicitly say so, he left the impression that Elway would never be the best quarterback in the game. Furious, Elway shot back. He claimed that Bradshaw had been jealous of him from the start, because he was envious about the huge contract ($12.7 million) Elway had received back in 1983. Just the same, Elway knew he had to prove himself on the football field.

In his previous two Super Bowl appearances, Elway had started off fast, only to falter in the second and third quarters. This time he never really got going. As mentioned, *Sports Illustrated* had called this the game between the puncher and the boxer, but they forgot to say that even a great puncher has bad days. Elway was off-target from the beginning, as the Broncos went three-and-out on their first series. After the 49ers got the ball, Montana led the San Francisco offense on a 66-yard scoring drive that gave them a 7-0 lead. Denver answered with a field goal, but the game was about to turn.

In contrast to Elway's slow start, Montana and the 49ers were at the top of their game. They had studied reels of film footage of the Broncos' defense and decided that Denver would probably not **blitz** Montana. They also recognized some key

ELWAY VERSUS MONTANA

John Elway and Joe Montana did not meet enough times over the years for commentators to build a consensus, so the question remains: Who was the better quarterback?

In terms of overall passing yardage, Elway comes out looking like the better quarterback. He was just the fourth quarterback in NFL history to exceed 50,000 passing yards, and he receives high marks for having played on a team that emphasized the rush over the pass—at least during the 1980s. He also posted more wins than Montana, with 148 in his career to Montana's 117.

In terms of precision, there is no doubt that Montana was better than Elway, and perhaps better than anyone else who ever played the game. Montana led the NFL in passer rating five times and set the all-time NFL mark on two occasions. He also has the fourth-highest passer rating in NFL history and tops Elway, 92.3 to 79.9, in that category, and has a better touchdown-to-interception ratio, 273-139 to 300-226, than the former Broncos quarterback.

Born and raised in western Pennsylvania (the same area as several quarterbacks who played in the NFL), Montana became the first true master of the West Coast offense. Established in the 1970s, this offense emphasizes short quarterback drops and quick passes. Rather than trying to throw the bomb (as Terry Bradshaw and John Elway did), the West Coast offense focuses on gradually moving the ball down the field via the short pass.

On any given day, Elway could have beaten Montana, and vice versa. The two men had great respect for each other. Sadly, their periods of greatness did not coincide, and fans will forever argue about which quarterback was better.

tendencies they could exploit. Thus, the 49ers would attack. This gave Montana plenty of time, and he was soon connecting with his favorite receiver, Jerry Rice. After the game, Montana explained what happened in a *Sports Illustrated* article:

> That's the thing about them. They kept following my eyes. Every time I looked somewhere, they over- played. They showed that on film, and they never changed. Actually, they never changed anything they showed on film.

That was unkind, to say the least. But Joe Montana was at least half right. The Broncos proved unable to figure out where he was going with the ball, and, consequently, he kept throw- ing it. After the 49ers recovered a fumble by Broncos running back Bobby Humphrey at midfield, they took over the game. Montana completed a seven-yard touchdown pass to tight end Brent Jones, fullback Tom Rathman scored from one yard out, and wide receiver Jerry Rice caught a 38-yard touchdown pass from Montana right before halftime, which made the score 27-3, and shattered the Broncos dreams yet again.

Elway played a little better in the second half, but he completed only 10 passes on the day for a total of 108 yards. Meanwhile, Montana completed 22 of 29 passes for 297 yards and a Super Bowl record five touchdowns. The 49ers racked up 461 yards of total offense and held the Broncos' rushing attack to just 64 yards. The final score said it all: 55-10. The 49ers had scored the most points in Super Bowl history, and the 45-point margin was the largest in Super Bowl history.

As the game wore on, the Broncos fought simply to prevent embarrassment, and they failed even in that. At one point, Elway slowly got to his feet after a devastating sack, only to be told by San Francisco **linebacker** Matt Millen not to let the team's disappointing performance get to him. Images of Elway

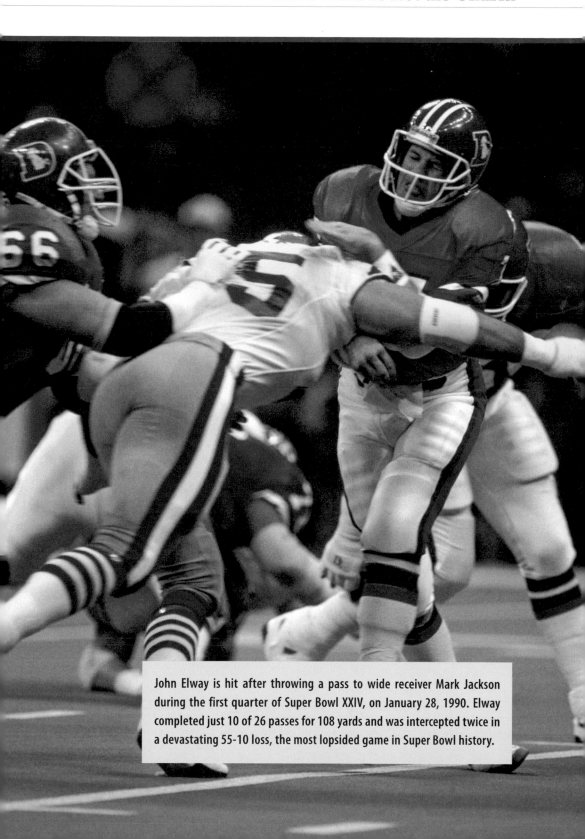

John Elway is hit after throwing a pass to wide receiver Mark Jackson during the first quarter of Super Bowl XXIV, on January 28, 1990. Elway completed just 10 of 26 passes for 108 yards and was intercepted twice in a devastating 55-10 loss, the most lopsided game in Super Bowl history.

either desperately running or being sacked abounded after the Super Bowl. Elway and the Broncos had hit rock bottom.

After the loss, many people offered their opinion of the beleaguered Broncos quarterback. For example, as recounted in *John Elway: Armed and Dangerous*, Johnny Unitas, who is generally considered the greatest quarterback of all time, said:

> My feeling about John Elway is that he has been, through-out his career, inconsistent. The reason he throws the ball so hard at times is because he doesn't anticipate the break of his receiver. . . . He's an extremely talented athlete, but I think that's the thing that bothers people. I thought his Super Bowl performance was very poor.

People refused to leave Elway alone after the game. Reporters continually asked him how it felt to have lost three Super Bowls in four years. For the most part, Elway answered all of the media's questions, but there were times when it seemed he had had enough. Although few people expected him simply to give up, many wondered how he would deal with the disappoint-ment. As he boarded the plane to return home, Elway told *Sports Illustrated*, "This is going to live with me. I know that."

That was the understatement of the year.

Lost Years

John Elway turned 30 in the summer after the mortifying Super Bowl loss to the 49ers. Like many other Americans at that age, he took some time to reflect. He had accomplished a good deal during those years. He retained his all-American good looks. He had more money than he ever could have imagined. He had a wonderful wife and three children—daughters Jessica and Jordan and son, Jack. (The Elways' fourth child, a daughter named Juliana, was not born until the following March.) But the humiliation of three Super Bowl losses, by a combined score of 136 to 40, stuck with him.

Many football commentators spent less time discussing Elway or the Broncos in the early 1990s. The man and the team seemed passé, as if their time had come and gone. The bigger story in the AFC was the Buffalo Bills, a team that made it to four straight Super Bowls and, to the mortification of quarterback Jim Kelly, lost all four of them. The Dallas Cowboys were also a better story than the Broncos. "America's Team," as they were called, the Cowboys made a major comeback in the 1990s, winning three Super Bowls.

Despite being shunted off to the side, Elway was not ready to call it quits. He would return to the game in 1990, and bide his time as the Broncos retooled.

A SEASON TO FORGET

The 1990 season was difficult enough in that the Broncos had to put the memory of Super Bowl XXIV behind them. But after the team got off to a 2–4 start, it seemed as if the Broncos began to unravel and could never fully get on track.

Denver started with a home loss to the Los Angeles Raiders, 14-9, then scratched out victories over Kansas City, 24-23, and Seattle, 34-31. The wheels began to come off on the last day of September, when the Broncos dropped a tough 29-28 decision to the Buffalo Bills, whose quarterback, Jim Kelly, seemed to have become the new comeback kid (Buffalo scored three touchdowns in the last two minutes of play!). After a difficult 30-29 loss to Cleveland and a 34-17 setback to Pittsburgh, the Broncos rebounded to beat the Indianapolis Colts, as Elway had one of his best games of the season, completing 20 of 31 passes for 317 yards and two touchdowns.

Then the unthinkable happened: The Broncos could not seem to win a game. During the final two months of the season, the Broncos went through one of the worst stretches in team history. Denver lost six straight games, including a disappointing 16-13 overtime loss to Chicago and an even more disheartening 31-20 defeat at the hands of Kansas City, in which Elway had his best game of the season—he completed 24 of 36 passes for 328 yards and two touchdowns. The season mercifully came to an end on December 30, with a 22-13 win over the Green Bay Packers. The Broncos posted a dismal 5–11 record, ensuring that they would finish last in the AFC West Division. For the Broncos, it was their worst season with Elway as quarterback. Despite the team's struggles, Elway completed 58.6 percent of his passes, the highest completion rate up to that point in his career.

A STEP FORWARD BEFORE A FEW STEPS BACK

The team seemed to come alive in 1991. The Broncos opened the season with a 45-14 win over the Cincinnati Bengals, which was their most lopsided opening-day victory in franchise history. They won three of their next four games, but a lopsided 42-14 loss to the Houston Oilers tempered the enthusiasm of Broncos fans. However, the team recovered to win 8 of its last 10 games to finish 12–4 on the season and capture its fifth AFC West Division crown in the last eight years.

The Broncos earned the second seed in the AFC and wound up hosting the Houston Oilers in the divisional round of the playoffs. The Broncos' players remembered what had happened in Week 6 in Houston, and they were eager to exact revenge on the Oilers. The Broncos quickly fell behind, 14-0, but were able to close the gap to 21-13 heading into halftime. In the second half, the Broncos' defense stiffened, as they held the Oilers to a field goal in the fourth quarter. Meanwhile, the Broncos kicked a field goal, and then Elway led an 80-yard drive to cut the Houston lead to 24-23 late in the fourth quarter. Then, in what would become known as "The Drive II," Elway guided the Broncos 77 yards in less than two minutes. With no timeouts left, Elway twice converted fourth-down plays on the drive, including a 44-yard completion to wide receiver Vance Johnson. Three plays later, kicker David Treadwell booted a 38-yard field goal to give the Broncos a 26-24 win. With the victory, Denver advanced to play in its fourth AFC Championship Game under Elway's watch. This time the foe was the Buffalo Bills.

Elway and Bills quarterback Jim Kelly were about the same age (they were both members of the famed Class of 1983), but they did not know each other well. Each man had experienced his fair share of adversity in attempting to get to the top, and sportscasters thought this championship game would be a shoot-out between two of the strongest-armed quarterbacks in the NFL. Instead, it turned into a defensive struggle, as the Broncos held the potent Bills' offense to just 213 total yards, 12 first downs, and one field goal. Unfortunately, Treadwell missed three field goals, and Elway threw a devastating interception that was returned by Bills linebacker Carlton Bailey for a touchdown. In the second half, Elway was knocked out of the game with a deep thigh bruise, and any hope of a comeback was dashed. Once again, the Broncos' dreams turned to dust.

OPENING UP THE OFFENSE

Before the 1992 season even got under way, the Broncos surprised everyone by selecting UCLA quarterback Tommy Maddox with their first-round pick in that year's draft. The Broncos' receiving corps was getting old by this time, so conventional wisdom said that Denver would pick a wide receiver with the twenty-fifth overall pick. This surprising development, along with the fact that Dan Reeves fired offensive coordinator Mike Shanahan during the off-season, drove a bigger wedge between Elway and the Broncos' head coach.

As for the 1992 season itself, the Broncos got off to a fast start, winning four of their first five games, including two fourth-quarter comeback victories against AFC West Division foes the Los Angeles Raiders and the Kansas City Chiefs. The Broncos won two of their next four games and stood at 6–3 heading into the back stretch of their schedule. But in Week 11, Elway injured his shoulder while running for a first down during the second quarter of Denver's game with the New York Giants. The Broncos won the game behind Maddox, but Elway was sidelined for the next four games. By the time Elway returned for a Week 16 contest with Seattle, the Broncos were 7–7 and basically out of the playoff hunt. Denver split its final two games to finish 8–8,

John Elway and Broncos head coach Dan Reeves chat during a practice session prior to Super Bowl XXIV. Unfortunately, the two never got along well, and after the 1992 season, Reeves's contract was not renewed by Broncos owner Pat Bowlen.

but many people in the organization wondered whether Dan Reeves was utilizing all of Elway's talents.

The answer to that question came on December 28, 1992, when Broncos owner Pat Bowlen announced that Dan Reeves's contract would not be renewed. Then, on January 25, 1993, Bowlen announced the hiring of Broncos defensive coordinator Wade Phillips as head coach. The son of Bum Phillips, the longtime coach of the Houston Oilers and New Orleans Saints, Wade brought a more relaxed style, which was a far cry from the regimented style of Dan Reeves. The Broncos seemed to have a new chance at glory, but they also knew that time was running out. John Elway was no longer the "kid" of 1983, nor even the veteran of 1990. He was now in his thirties, and if Denver ever wanted to ride his golden arm to the Super Bowl, it had to act fast.

The first year under Phillips was good for Elway, but the team struggled at times and finished 9–7 in the regular season. They did, however, qualify for the playoffs, where they lost in the wild-card round to their AFC West Division foe the Los Angeles Raiders, 42-24. As for Elway, he had his best season

DAN REEVES

To say that Denver's head coach and quarterback had "issues" is to put it mildly. John Elway and Dan Reeves were sometimes friendly, sometimes cool, and sometimes they seemed more like enemies than members of the same unit.

Born in Rome, Georgia, in 1944, Reeves was 16 years older than Elway and had played running back for the Dallas Cowboys from 1965 to 1972. After serving as an assistant coach with the Cowboys, the 37-year-old Reeves became head coach of the Broncos in 1981. When Elway was drafted by the Broncos in 1983, the two seemed on good terms. Reeves showed a lot of confidence in his young quarterback, starting him during his rookie season, and he backed Elway even when the press questioned his ability.

The two did not have much in common, however. Their differences were evident during press conferences, and on the field, where Elway preferred a pass-first offense, while Reeves liked to focus on the running game. In Dallas, Reeves had learned under Tom Landry, who preferred a ball-control style of play. Throughout the late 1980s, Elway felt that Reeves was depriving him—and the team—of the benefit of taking

to date. He was named AFC Offensive Player of the Year after leading the conference in passing yards (4,030), completion percentage (63.2 percent), passer rating (92.8), and touchdown passes (25). In addition, he led the NFL in pass attempts (551) and completions (348). Elway excelled under new offensive coordinator Jim Fassel, who also had coached Elway at Stanford, but the quarterback's offensive explosion did not translate to victories. Surprisingly, the Broncos' seven losses came by a

advantage of Elway's passing ability, akin to what Dan Marino was doing with the Miami Dolphins.

After the three Super Bowl defeats, Reeves's and Elway's relationship deteriorated even more. Neither man ever publicly blamed the other, but there was plenty of bad blood between the two. As a result, Elway was undoubtedly pleased when Broncos owner Pat Bowlen did not renew Reeves's contract after the 1992 season.

However, Reeves was not finished—far from it. He coached the New York Giants from 1993 to 1996, earning Associated Press Coach of the Year honors in his first season when he led the team to an 11–5 record and a berth in the playoffs. He was then fired after the 1996 season and became head coach of the Atlanta Falcons in 1997. In 1998, he again was named coach of the year when he led the Falcons to an amazing 14–2 record and a trip to the Super Bowl. Unfortunately, he was unable to maintain that success and near the end of the 2003 season, he was fired again. During his 23 years as an NFL head coach, Reeves was 190–165–2, including an 11–9 mark in postseason play.

mere 30 points. For some reason, the comeback kid could not get the Broncos over the hump in 1993. Unfortunately, 1994 would be even more disappointing.

Denver started the 1994 season with *four* losses in a row: to San Diego, 37-34; the New York Jets, 25-22; the Los Angeles Raiders, 48-16; and the Buffalo Bills, 27-20. The last of these defeats was showcased on Monday Night Football, and astute commentators began to say that Elway was past his prime. Although the Broncos seemingly turned things around with seven wins in their next nine games, including a 20-15 victory over the San Diego Chargers—the team that would represent the AFC in the Super Bowl—the season essentially came to an end in Week 14 against the Chiefs. Although Elway helped lead the Broncos to victory with a gaudy 130.3 passer rating, he strained his left knee late in the game, and he could not play in two of the Broncos' final three games. Consequently, Denver ended the season by losing its last three games, including a 42-19 defeat at the hands of the San Francisco 49ers, that year's Super Bowl champion.

PLANTING THE SEEDS

After a combined mark of 16–16 in 1993 and 1994, Coach Wade Phillips was fired at the end of the 1994 season. Then, on January 31, 1995, the Mike Shanahan era officially began, as Broncos owner Pat Bowlen announced the hiring of the San Francisco 49ers' offensive coordinator as the Broncos' new head coach.

Shanahan had been closely connected with Elway at several points in their respective careers. Shanahan had first been the quarterbacks coach, then the offensive coordinator for the Broncos in the mid-1980s before he left to become head coach of the Los Angeles Raiders. He then again served as quarterbacks coach in Denver from 1989 to 1991 before heading to San Francisco, where he was the 49ers' offensive coordinator from 1992 to 1994 and learned the West Coast offense under Head Coach George Seifert.

Elway and Shanahan had always connected well, largely because Shanahan (unlike Dan Reeves) had wanted to utilize Elway's strong arm and passing ability as much as possible. Conflicts between Shanahan and Reeves had prevented the team from maximizing its potential in the 1980s, but when Shanahan took over as head coach, many things changed, and most were for the better.

Shanahan described the Broncos' situation when he took over in 1995 in his book *Think Like a Champion*:

> The makeup of our team was not what I wanted it to be. And at that time I was concerned. The year before, the Broncos' offense allowed 55 sacks—27th in the 28-team league. They lost 18 fumbles—25th in the league. They rushed for only 1,470 yards—23rd in the league. Defensively they were even worse. They allowed 396 points—26th in the league; 5,907 total yards—28th in the league; and 4,155 passing yards—dead last!

One might ask: Why did Shanahan agree to return to Denver? First and foremost, he knew the team well. Second, he loved a challenge. Shanahan possessed a fierce work ethic, which he instilled in his players. Before long, Broncos players were working out harder and longer than any of their opponents. The results showed; in just his second season with the Broncos, Shanahan had vastly improved the team. He described the improvements in *Think Like a Champion*: "In 1996, we finished with 1,995 rushing yards—5th in the NFL—and we allowed only 3,298 passing yards—8th in the league."

LEAVING MEDIOCRITY BEHIND

The 1995 season was a transition period for the Denver Broncos, but there were signs that the team was moving in the right direction. The Broncos split their first eight games, as Elway threw for more than 300 yards three times. In a

38-31 win over the Washington Redskins, he completed 30 of 47 passes for 327 yards and two touchdowns, including a 43-yard Hail Mary pass that found rookie wide receiver Rod Smith in the end zone as time expired. Four weeks later, Elway and the Broncos showed how dominant they could be, whipping the Oakland Raiders, 27-0, on Monday Night Football. Elway completed 23 of 46 passes for 324 yards and two touchdowns in the win.

MIKE SHANAHAN

Born in suburban Oak Park, Illinois, Mike Shanahan had been a promising quarterback at Eastern Illinois University, until one of his kidneys was ruptured during practice, which prematurely ended his playing career. Turning to coaching, Shanahan had worked his way up the college coaching ranks, serving as offensive coordinator at the University of Florida in the early 1980s before accepting a job with the Denver Broncos as quarterbacks coach in 1984.

Intense and driven, Shanahan helped tutor a young John Elway in 1984 and 1985, and then was promoted by Coach Dan Reeves to offensive coordinator in 1986. After the 1987 season, he left to become head coach of the Los Angeles Raiders. He spent less than two years there before Raiders owner Al Davis fired him after the fourth game of the 1989 season. He then came back to Denver to serve as quarterbacks coach for a couple more seasons before departing for the San Francisco 49ers. Shanahan absorbed the West Coast offense while in San Francisco and returned to the Broncos in 1995 after Wade Phillips was fired.

The Broncos' new head coach did not have any great surprises up his sleeve, no tantalizing changes in store for

The second half of the 1995 slate was similar to the first half; the Broncos were up and down. One week, they overwhelmed the Arizona Cardinals, 38-6, the next week they were thrashed by the Philadelphia Eagles, 31-13. The Broncos finished the season 8–8, but Elway had shown flashes of his former self, leading Denver to three fourth-quarter comebacks and throwing a career-high 26 touchdown passes. More important, the

the offense; rather, he insisted on concentrating on the fundamentals, day in and day out. The Broncos had become somewhat complacent in the early 1990s, with some players missing practice and others not giving their all. Shanahan put a stop to that, insisting that each player make it to practice every day and that he give his full effort at practice. He also had an eye for new, young talent; shortly after Shanahan took over, he drafted Terrell ("TD") Davis in the sixth round of the 1995 draft. Davis would go on to become a three-time Pro Bowl player and was a cornerstone of the 1997 and 1998 Broncos teams.

Shanahan later wrote a book in 1999 entitled *Think Like a Champion: Building Success One Victory at a Time*, which explains his coaching method and is sprinkled with admiring comments from players as different as Deion Sanders and Matt Millen. In the book, Shanahan expresses confidence that every person can attain his or her goals if he or she would only work hard and long enough: "Of course, there's a little caveat. As Sean Connery said to Kevin Costner in *The Untouchables*, 'What are you prepared to do?'" Under Mike Shanahan, the Broncos were prepared to do more than ever before.

Denver head coach Mike Shanahan and John Elway discuss strategy during the first quarter of the Broncos' opening game of the 1995 season, a 22-7 win over the Buffalo Bills. Although the Broncos finished a disappointing 8–8 that year, Elway set career highs in touchdown passes (26) and 300-yard games (5).

Broncos had found the makings of a potent running attack, as rookie tailback Terrell Davis rushed for 1,117 yards and seven touchdowns in 14 games.

The 1996 regular season was the Broncos' best since 1984, Elway's second year in the league. Much like that season, however, Denver's 1996 campaign came to a disappointing end. The Broncos started the season well, beating the New York Jets, 31-6; Seattle, 30-20; and Tampa Bay, 27-23, in workingman-like fashion. Then came the first loss, a painful 17-14 setback to the Kansas City Chiefs, as Denver gave up a fourth-quarter lead in Elway's worst performance of the season. But Denver got right back on track, beating Cincinnati, 14-10; San Diego, 28-17; Baltimore, 45-34; and Kansas City, 34-7. At this point, it appeared that the Broncos had bucked the trend of starting out slow, which had occurred during the previous three seasons. The win over the Chargers was especially gratifying for Elway, as he torched San Diego for 28 unanswered points, after the Broncos had fallen behind, 17-0. Elway completed 32 of 41 passes for 323 yards and four touchdowns, including three to **All-Pro** tight end Shannon Sharpe.

In Week 10, the Broncos continued their winning ways, beating Oakland, 22-21, on Monday Night Football. The win included another thrilling last-minute drive by Elway, as he connected on a 49-yard scoring strike to Rod Smith to cap a six-play, 73-yard drive. From there the Broncos won their next four: defeating the Chicago Bears, 17-12; the New England Patriots, 34-8; the Minnesota Vikings, 21-17; and the Seattle Seahawks, 34-7. By now Denver fans were jubilant, but their elation was quieted by a thrashing delivered by the Green Bay Packers, who silenced Mile High Stadium with a 41-6 win. Brett Favre, Green Bay's All-Pro quarterback, passed for 280 yards and played like a young John Elway. Granted, Elway was given the week off by Shanahan, because the Broncos had already clinched the AFC West Division and home-field advantage in the playoffs, but it was a tough loss to take, nonetheless. The Broncos quickly put the humiliating loss to the eventual Super Bowl champions behind them and defeated Oakland, 24-19. As most of the starters watched from the sideline, the Broncos wrapped up the season with a 16-10 loss to San Diego. When all was said and done, the Denver Broncos had compiled a 13–3 record and were, for the first time since 1991, division champions.

Redemption was at hand. Having posted the best record in the AFC, the Broncos hosted the Jacksonville Jaguars in the divisional round of the playoffs. The Jaguars were only in their second year as an NFL franchise. With a 9–7 record, they had snuck into the playoffs as a wild card. Denver was installed as a 14-point favorite, and the Broncos fans at Mile High Stadium had to be confident entering the game.

The Broncos scored 12 points in the first quarter, but their ground game petered out after that. The Jaguars came roaring back with 13 second-quarter and seven third-quarter points, all unanswered. They then added a field goal in the beginning of the fourth quarter, to take a commanding 23-12 lead. With about 11 minutes left in the game, Elway finally got the offense back on track by leading a nine-play, 57-yard touchdown drive that cut the Jaguars lead to 23-20, after the Broncos converted a two-point conversion attempt. However, Jacksonville quarterback Mark Brunell responded with a touchdown drive of his own, pushing the Jaguars' lead to 30-20 with 3:39 left in the game. Yet again Elway responded, driving the Broncos 80 yards in less than two minutes, as he capped the drive with a 15-yard touchdown pass to wide receiver Ed McCaffrey. Unfortunately, the magic ended there: The Jaguars recovered Jason Elam's onside kick and the game was over.

The Broncos and their fans were shocked. During the next few months, Elway was repeatedly asked what had gone wrong and how he would deal with it. On one occasion, as he recounted in *John Elway: Armed and Dangerous*, he came as close to brutal honesty as professional athletes ever do:

> I haven't committed hara-kiri yet, but I've thought about it for a month. I'm not sure I'll ever get over it. That's as disappointed as I've ever been. You can talk

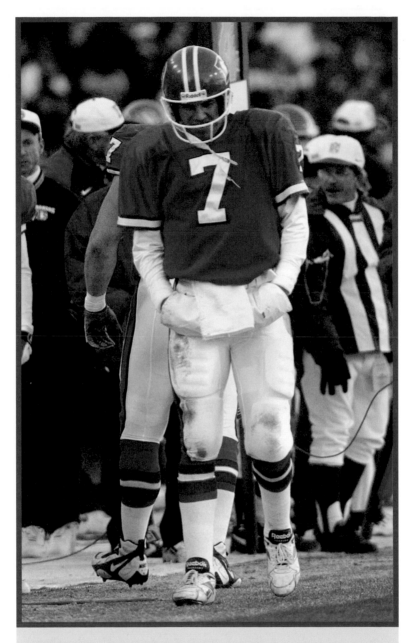

John Elway shows his disappointment as he paces the sidelines during Denver's AFC divisional-round playoff game with the Jacksonville Jaguars on January 4, 1997. Despite being overwhelming favorites to win the game, the Broncos suffered a disappointing 30-27 defeat at the hands of the Jaguars, who finished just 9–7 that season.

about the Super Bowl losses or anything. There's not one that comes close to this.

Meanwhile, Brett Favre and the Green Bay Packers sailed through the NFC Championship Game and went to the Super Bowl, where they played the New England Patriots, a team Denver had beaten 34-8 during the regular season. The Packers won, 35-21, and many observers started to say that a new Green Bay dynasty (the first had been under Head Coach Vince Lombardi in the 1960s) had arrived. For Denver and John Elway, it was the worst of times, as they watched their hopes for glory disappear into the shadows of that early January evening. Even the most ardent of Broncos fans had to ask themselves: Would the chance come again?

ELWAY WRITES A BOOK

Football players are not often known for their literary acumen; for example, famed Oakland Raiders coach John Madden parodied himself with the title of his 1984 *Hey, Wait a Minute (I Wrote a Book)!*, which was actually considered a rather good one. But in 1997, John Elway published his first book. Cowritten with Greg Brown, *Comeback Kid* was an effort to inspire young people to try harder in the face of adversity.

Elway started out by describing his father and family, the most important influences in his life. He praised his father, who had always been his athletic inspiration, and he wrote in *Comeback Kid* of how competitive all the family members had been:

> In school, we'd compete to see who could get the best grades (I earned A's and B's and never got a C until I went to college). . . . The most intense family battles, however, involved board games. We'd play Risk for days. . . . Finally my parents had to outlaw the game in our house for family sanity.

Given that the Elways were such a competitive bunch, how did John Elway handle losing three Super Bowls? He offered an explanation in *Comeback Kid*:

> The fact that we led at halftime in the first two Super Bowls [sic] only made the pain deeper. My only consolation has been that I've walked off three Super Bowl fields knowing that I tried and did everything I possibly could to win.

John's wife, Janet, provided deeper context on the matter. Only a wife could know the immensity of the pain involved with these losses in the biggest game in professional football, but she reported in *Comeback Kid* that,

> I was amazed how well John handled the Super Bowl losses. I could tell he was really sad. I know he really wanted to win. We all went to dinner after one of them, and John comforted everyone else. He took the attitude that there are worse things in life that could happen.

No one knows how many young people read *Comeback Kid*, but one suspects that those who did began to see Elway as an all-round hero, one who could be admired for the way he handled wins and loses, and the way he *played* the game.

The Best Is Yet to Come

At the beginning of the 1997 season, the Denver Broncos were raring to get back out onto the field. No one on the team needed to be reminded of the painful playoff defeat at the hands of the Jacksonville Jaguars. Coach Mike Shanahan had pushed, prodded, and developed his players to where they thought they had a chance to make another run in the playoffs—and they were determined not to let another "Big Moment" or "Big Game" slip away.

But before the regular season even began, the campaign was almost derailed when Elway suffered an apparent torn right bicep tendon in an August 4 preseason contest against the Miami Dolphins in Mexico City. Many Broncos fans wondered if Elway would make it for the season opener; fortunately, their fears were allayed when he trotted onto the field less than three weeks later in their final preseason game against the San Francisco 49ers on August 23.

Denver opened the regular season by beating the Chiefs—at Kansas City—19-3. Elway was not spectacular, but he did throw for 246 yards in the win. The Broncos followed the opening-week win by defeating Seattle, 35-14; the St. Louis Rams, 35-14; Cincinnati, 38-20; Atlanta, 29-21; and New England, 34-13, to start the season 6–0 heading into their bye week. The win streak was highlighted by an interesting matchup with former Broncos coach Dan Reeves, who was now the head coach of the Atlanta Falcons. Elway threw for 243 yards and three touchdowns in the win.

After the bye week, the Broncos dropped their first game of the season, 28-25, to the Oakland Raiders. Elway passed for 309 yards in the loss, but the big story of the day was Raiders coach Joe Bugel's mocking rendition of the "Mile High Salute," a military-like greeting given to Broncos fans by running back Terrell Davis after he scored a touchdown.

That loss seemed to rev up the Broncos. They rattled off three straight wins, beating Buffalo, 23-20; Seattle, 30-27; and the Carolina Panthers, 34-0. Denver looked almost invincible before dropping a close one to Kansas City, 24-22, as Chiefs kicker Pete Stoyanovich booted a 54-yarder as time expired. There were two more appearances on Monday Night Football that season: Denver thrashed Oakland, 31-3, as Terrell Davis delivered his fair share of Mile High Salutes in a three-touchdown effort; but the Broncos dropped a painful 34-17 decision to the San Francisco 49ers, as Elway had his worst game of the season, completing just 16 of 41 passes for 150 yards and tossing two interceptions. The loss to the 49ers not only ended any hope of capturing the top seed in the AFC but also winning the AFC West Division title. Despite closing the season with a 38-3 rout of San Diego, the Broncos finished 12–4 and would have to settle for the fourth seed in the AFC.

John Elway directs a pass to fullback Howard Griffith during the Broncos' 30-27 win over the Seattle Seahawks on November 2, 1997. In the victory, Elway completed 19 of 30 passes for 252 yards and two touchdowns, but he also became just the second quarterback in NFL history to top the 50,000-yard mark in total offense.

THE PLAYOFFS

The Broncos' stellar 1997 season reflected well on Mike Shanahan's coaching style, but the two losses late in the season cost Denver the opportunity to have home-field advantage throughout the playoffs. As a wild-card team, Denver played first against the Jacksonville Jaguars, who had knocked them out of the playoffs the year before. The Broncos were eager to exact revenge on the Jaguars, and it did not take long to see that they would have no trouble doing so. Denver jumped out to a 21-0 lead and cruised to a 42-17 win behind 310 rushing yards, 184 of which came from Terrell Davis. Then it was on to Kansas City for yet another game against the Chiefs.

Under Marty Schottenheimer's guidance, the Chiefs had greatly improved; in fact, they split their two games with the Broncos that season and edged Denver with a 13–3 record to take the AFC West Division title. Games in Arrowhead Stadium were almost always hotly contested, and this was no exception. As they had against Jacksonville, Denver used a ball-control offense, as Elway threw the ball just 19 times. Led by 101 yards from Terrell Davis, Denver's rushing attack carried the day. Nonetheless, Elway again led a fourth-quarter comeback, driving the Broncos 49 yards on six plays to give Denver a 14-10 win. With the victory, the Broncos would be heading to their first AFC Championship Game in six years.

With a berth in Super Bowl XXXII on the line, the Broncos traveled to Three Rivers Stadium in Pittsburgh to face the Steelers, a team that had beaten them 35-24 during the regular season. The Broncos jumped out to a 24-14 halftime lead behind two touchdown passes from Elway. In the second half, Denver played a bit more conservatively and relied on its defense to win the game. The plan worked for most of the final 30 minutes, but the Steelers were able to cut the Broncos' lead to 24-21 on a Kordell Stewart 14-yard touchdown pass to receiver Charles Johnson with just 2:46 left in the game. But Elway was able to complete a huge third-and-six play with two minutes left in the game, and the Broncos ran out the clock. For the first time in eight years, the Broncos were headed to the Super Bowl.

SUPER BOWL XXXII

Brett Favre and the Green Bay Packers were heavy favorites (11.5 points) to win Super Bowl XXXII, and given the Broncos' terrible track record in the big game, not many experts and fans thought they had a chance. Favre, who appeared to have modeled some aspects of his game on Elway's, had been the NFC's Most Valuable Player the last two seasons (and would soon make it three). In 1997, he led the NFL with 35 touchdown passes and was second in the league in passing yards with 3,867. His Packers had humbled the New England Patriots in Super Bowl XXXI, which left some people talking

MARTY SCHOTTENHEIMER

Many players, teams, and coaches have faced John Elway's mighty right arm, but few have had to deal with the gunslinger as often as Marty Schottenheimer. If not for Elway's fourth-quarter magic, Schottenheimer may have actually won a Super Bowl or two, or, at the very least, made it to a Super Bowl.

Born in Canonsburg, Pennsylvania, in 1943, Schottenheimer played at the University of Pittsburgh before going on to a six-year NFL career at linebacker, with Buffalo and the Boston Patriots. Turning to coaching after his playing days were over, Schottenheimer worked his way up the ranks to become head coach of the Cleveland Browns in 1984, just one year after John Elway arrived in Denver. The two were destined for many a shoot-out.

Cleveland won the AFC Central Division in 1986, 1987, and 1989, but the team was denied further glory by Elway and the Denver Broncos, who beat the Browns for the AFC title in 1986, 1987, and 1989. ("The Drive" was during the first of these games.) Whether he was trying to get the upper hand on Elway and the Broncos or not (especially because he was 0–4 against the Broncos with Elway at quarterback), Schottenheimer left Cleveland to become head coach of the Kansas City Chiefs after the 1988 season.

about a new dynasty. Favre was not the entire show, however; he was just the best of the bunch.

The Packers had the largest player in professional football. Some people said **defensive tackle** Gilbert Brown was 345 pounds, while others compared him to a medium-sized SUV (sport utility vehicle). Green Bay also had an explosive wide

The Chiefs and the Broncos had long been fierce rivals, but the rivalry only grew stronger with the arrival of Schottenheimer, who turned the Chiefs into a perennial playoff contender. Before Schottenheimer arrived, the Chiefs had only made it to the postseason once in the previous 17 years. After an 8–7–1 finish in 1989, he led the Chiefs to 11–5 in 1990 and two straight 10–6 finishes in 1991 and 1992, but the Chiefs finished second in the AFC West Division all three years. More important, his struggles with Elway continued. Schottenheimer posted a 2–6 record against the Broncos from 1989 to 1992. The Broncos and their star quarterback just seemed to play better when they faced the Chiefs. The two teams met four times on Monday Night Football, with each team winning twice. As for the postseason, the Chiefs and Broncos only met once during the Schottenheimer/Elway era: a 14-10 Denver win in the divisional round of the 1997 playoffs. One can sympathize with Marty Schottenheimer, who was fired by the Chargers in early 2007, after 20 years as head coach at Cleveland, Kansas City, Washington, and San Diego, and perhaps agree that much of the Denver Broncos' success during John Elway's career came at the expense of the Schottenheimer-led Cleveland Browns and Kansas City Chiefs.

receiver tandem, in Antonio Freeman and Robert Brooks, both of whom had more than 1,000 receiving yards. The Packers were also strong on the ground, as running back Dorsey Levens had rushed for 1,435 yards. On defense, the Packers were led by All-Pro defensive end Reggie White, who had 11 sacks that season. On top of all this talent, the Packers had had their way with the Broncos the year before, beating them 41-6 behind Favre's 280 yards passing and four touchdowns.

Denver pinned its hopes on three men: Elway, Coach Shanahan, and running back Terrell Davis. But for the Broncos to pull off an upset, they would have to get something extra out of each and every man on the team, and that was where Coach Shanahan excelled. When the whistle blew on January 25, 1998, Shanahan did not have to exhort his players or shout at them to motivate them. They were ready, by virtue of the demanding practices he had put them through all year.

Days before the game, the *New York Times* ran a special Super Bowl section entitled "Who'll Stop the Reign?" The NFC had won 13 Super Bowls *in a row*, and Elway's Denver Broncos had lost three of them. Most commentators thought it would be an interesting showdown between the league's new gunslinger (Favre) and its old gunslinger (Elway), but most experts thought Green Bay would prevail.

Super Bowl XXXII was played at Qualcomm Stadium in San Diego, where light, airy breezes favored the strong passing games of both John Elway and Brett Favre. Before the game began, Favre had been asked if he secretly hoped Elway would win the Super Bowl that had so long been denied him. Favre gave an honest answer, saying that he would root for Elway if he were not playing the Packers.

Favre started off in typical fashion. The three-time MVP moved his team smartly down the field; eight plays later, Antonio Freeman hauled in a 22-yard pass from Favre in the end zone, giving the Packers a 7-0 lead. But Elway came right back with a 10-play, 58-yard drive, capped by a 1-yard Terrell

John Elway crosses the goal line for a touchdown during the second quarter of Super Bowl XXXII, on January 25, 1998. Elway's score gave the Broncos a 14-7 lead over the Green Bay Packers and catapulted Denver to its first Super Bowl victory in franchise history.

Davis touchdown run. For the first time in Super Bowl history, each team had scored on its initial possession.

Then, on what was to be the last play of the first quarter, disaster struck. Terrell Davis was hit hard by an opposing player. He lurched off the field, looking dazed. Coach Shanahan was alarmed. Davis was the heart and soul of Denver's offense, and without him it would be difficult for the Broncos to win the game. Talking with Davis on the sideline, Shanahan realized that his All-Pro running back was going to be out of action, at least for a while. Then he asked for a supreme sacrifice.

Knowing that Davis could not see (he was temporarily blinded by a migraine headache), Shanahan asked him to go back into the game, as a decoy, so the Green Bay Packers would *think* Davis was still going to run. There was no threat to

TERRELL "TD" DAVIS

Born in San Diego in 1972, Terrell Davis had a difficult upbringing. He had an alcoholic father and his mother was busy dealing with Terrell's five older brothers. Mrs. Davis held the family together, though, and Terrell soon discovered his passion for sports of all kinds (over the years, football came to dominate).

Davis went to Lincoln Prep Academy and then to Long Beach State University for one year. After the 1991 season, Long Beach dropped its football program, and Davis transferred to the University of Georgia, which, in the past, had produced great running backs such as Herschel Walker.

Davis's career at Georgia was not spectacular. He rushed for just 445 yards during his senior season, largely due to a torn hamstring. In addition, he and his coach, Ray Goff, did not get along, and Davis claimed that Goff had made him practice while he was injured. Despite his problems, Davis was selected by the Denver Broncos in the sixth round of the 1995 NFL draft. He had hoped to be picked higher and many experts gave him little chance to make the Broncos' roster. But Coach Shanahan saw something in Davis, something that others overlooked. First, there was his fantastic physique; second, there was his tremendous desire to succeed. Although he entered training camp as the sixth-string running back, Davis worked hard, and by the end of the preseason he impressed the coaches enough that he was named the starting running back for the Broncos' opener with Buffalo.

Davis's health; Coach Shanahan was not going to risk his prized running back's future.

Davis staggered back onto the field, and the Packers prepared for a run. The ball was at the Green Bay 1-yard line. It

Davis rushed for 1,117 yards in 1995, but really turned it on in 1996 and 1997. His 1,538 rushing yards in 1996 were good for second in the league behind Detroit Lions running back Barry Sanders, and Davis also finished second in total yards with 1,848. Not only strong but fast, he "saw" holes in defensive lines and exploited them better than anyone else in the game. Time and again he rushed for more than 100 yards a game, and by the end of 1997 he had amassed 1,750 yards on the ground, which again was second behind Sanders. He also tied for the league lead with 15 rushing touchdowns. In 1998, he not only led the league in rushing (2,008 yards) but also rushing touchdowns (21). In Super Bowl XXXIII, played on January 31, 1999, Davis became the first player in NFL history to rush for more than 100 yards in seven straight postseason games.

Yet throughout his short-lived career, Davis was battling an inner enemy: migraine headaches. They were so bad in his teens that he thought he would go blind, and they were not properly diagnosed until his college years. Despite the migraines, Davis's career was ultimately cut short by another health issue. During the fourth game of the 1999 season, Davis tore both his anterior cruciate and medial collateral ligaments in his right knee. Although he returned the following year, a stress fracture kept him out of all but five games. In 2001, he had to have arthroscopic surgery on both of his knees, which forced him to retire during the 2002 preseason.

would have been an easy run for Davis if he had been healthy, but on this occasion Elway faked the **handoff** to Davis and then ran all the way to the right side of the field on a **bootleg**, making it into the end zone himself! The Broncos took their first lead, 14-7.

After Jason Elam kicked a 51-yard field goal to make it 17-7, the Packers answered right before halftime with an amazing 17-play, 95-yard drive, capped by a six-yard touch-down pass from Favre to tight end Mark Chmura. Green Bay then tied the game early in the third quarter with a 27-yard field goal. Elway and the Broncos then broke the tie with a 13-play, 92-yard drive, which was highlighted by a 36-yard pass from Elway to receiver Ed McCaffrey. Then, facing a third-and-six from the Packers' 12-yard line, Elway would have to come up big. During the course of the past two years, no team had been tougher in these situations than Green Bay, and the tension was evident. Could Denver succeed where it had failed so often in the past?

Getting the snap, Elway dropped back to pass, but he found no open receivers. Relying on a tactic he had learned from his father so many years ago, he faked a pass, then ran toward the right side of the end zone. The Packers were not fooled, and three Green Bay defenders converged to meet him near the 9-yard line. Safeties LeRoy Butler and Mike Prior, along with linebacker Brian Williams, were known as hard hitters, but Elway put his head down and charged forward. Perhaps the smart thing would have been to run out of bounds, stop the clock, and allow Coach Shanahan to decide whether he wanted to have Jason Elam kick a field goal. But Elway wanted to win; he did not want to settle for a field goal. Rather than run toward the sideline, he leaped into the air, was hit hard by Butler, and began to spin like a helicopter through the air. Luckily, his momentum carried him far enough to land for the first down!

This was the defining moment of the game. Elway's daring gained his team the first down, and two plays later Terrell

Davis ran in from one yard out to give the Broncos a 24-17 lead. Tight end Shannon Sharpe declared, "When I saw him do that and then get up pumping his fist, I said, "'It's on.' That's when I was sure we were going to win." But there was more football to be played.

During the third quarter, Green Bay safety Eugene Robinson's voice was the loudest on the field, and on the sidelines. A talented player who had intercepted Elway a number of times over the years (prior to joining the Packers, he had played for the Seattle Seahawks), Robinson was seen exhorting his teammates, saying things such as, "They are not a great team, they are not even a good one, they don't belong on the same field with us!" Some commentators had phrased this more politely in the lead-up to the Super Bowl, but few believed it now.

After the Broncos took the lead, Favre came right back with an inspired drive that began as time was running out in the third quarter. Keyed by a 39-yard reception by Antonio Freeman, the Packers were soon on the Broncos' doorstep. Not quite a minute and a half into the fourth quarter, Favre hit Freeman again, this time for a 13-yard touchdown that knotted the game at 24-24.

For the remainder of the fourth quarter, the two teams traded possessions but neither team could maneuver close enough to score. Then with about three and a half minutes left, the Broncos took over with one last chance to win the game before heading to overtime. These were the moments when Elway was at his best, and he had one more mountain to climb in order to achieve his ultimate goal.

Taking over around midfield, Elway calmly directed the Broncos downfield. After a 15-yard personal foul on the Packers, Elway hit fullback Howard Griffith for a 23-yard completion. On the next play, Terrell Davis scored on an eight-yard run. However, it was called back due to a **holding** penalty. Davis, though, was not going to be denied. He again got the ball

John Elway is carried off the field by his teammates after the Broncos defeated the Green Bay Packers, 31-24, in Super Bowl XXXII. After 15 seasons in the NFL and three previous trips to the Big Game, Elway had finally led Denver to that elusive Super Bowl title.

and carried it for 17 yards to the Green Bay 1-yard line. Just about everyone at the game and those watching on television expected Davis would get the ball. He did, and went untouched into the end zone for his third touchdown of the game. The Broncos were now up, 31-24, with 1:45 left in the game. Only later was it revealed that the Green Bay coaches had decided to let Davis score so that they had enough time to come back and tie the game.

After the kickoff, Favre had to lead the Packers 70 yards in 1:39. Like Elway, Favre was a master at leading his team to comeback wins, but he had never played a game under such intense pressure. Favre completed two key pass plays to get the

Packers down to the Denver 35-yard line with a little more than a minute left on the clock. After a swing pass gained four yards on first down, Favre threw two straight incompletions to set up a fourth-and-six at the Denver 31. The Green Bay quarterback then tried to find tight end Mark Chmura, but the ball was batted down by Broncos linebacker John Mobley. Denver then took over and Elway ran out the clock.

Everyone who ever commented on what happened that day agrees that the Denver sideline simply erupted when the game ended. Denver had WON! The Broncos had been to four Super Bowls in the past (1978, 1987, 1988, 1990), but they had come up empty in each one. Now Denver had won the BIG GAME!

Minutes later, John Elway stood atop the podium on the field, grinning from ear to ear, while Broncos owner Pat Bowlen hoisted the Lombardi Trophy in the air. The irony that Vince Lombardi was the coach behind the Green Bay Packers dynasty of the 1960s was lost on no one. Holding the trophy high, Bowlen yelled: "I've only got four words . . . This one's for JOHN!!"

Unfinished Business

In the history of the NFL, there has seldom been a celebration quite as intense as the one that followed the Broncos' victory in Super Bowl XXXII. The curse had been broken; a spell had been lifted; and Denver was on top of the world. But what about the main man, number seven? Only years later was it revealed that, the night he cleaned out his locker after the Super Bowl win in January 1998, John Elway turned to teammate Shannon Sharpe and said, "I'm coming back."

ONE LAST TIME

Elway did indeed return for his sixteenth season with the Broncos. In an era when many players moved from one team to another—lured by high salaries and incentives—Elway had played his entire career in one city. Fortunately, most of the

John Elway scrambles downfield during the Broncos' 27-21 win over the New England Patriots in Week 1 of the 1998 season. In the last home opener of Elway's career, he completed 22 of 34 passes for 257 yards and a touchdown.

core players on the Super Bowl champion Broncos did the same. Of the 22 starters from the 1997 season, the Broncos only lost two players to free agency—right guard Brian Habib and middle linebacker Allen Aldridge. As Coach Shanahan put it, the Broncos wanted to repeat, to show that their big win was not a fluke.

As defending champions, the Broncos got to start their season in grand style, with an appearance on Monday Night Football. Denver took on the Patriots at Mile High Stadium, and though New England proved tougher than expected, Denver came out on top, 27-21. Another home game followed, as Denver welcomed the Dallas Cowboys, who were coming off a season in which they missed the playoffs for the first time in seven years. This was a high-scoring affair, with Denver out-gunning Dallas, 42-23, as Elway threw for 268 yards and two touchdowns.

By now some experts were starting to talk about a possible Denver dynasty, but it was too early in the season for self-congratulation. The Broncos then traveled to Oakland, where they defeated the Raiders, 34-17. Unfortunately, Elway injured his shoulder during the game, but backup Bubby Brister filled in admirably in wins against the Washington Redskins, 38-16, and the Philadelphia Eagles, 41-16. Anyone who looked at the offensive numbers had to be startled by how many points Denver was racking up and the team's margin of victory.

After they dispatched Seattle, 21-16, behind 208 yards rushing from Terrell Davis, the Broncos had a bye week and could reenergize after their 6–0 start. The following week, Elway had his best game of the season up to that point, leading the Broncos to a 37-24 win over the Jacksonville Jaguars. The Denver quarterback passed for 295 yards, but the highlight of the game came when kicker Jason Elam booted a 63-yard field goal, which tied the NFL record, set by Tom Dempsey in 1970.

In Week 9, Denver traveled to Cincinnati to face the Bengals. Again, Elway worked his fourth-quarter magic, as he drove the Broncos 53 yards in less than two minutes for a game-clinching touchdown and a 33-26 win. Elway was, of course, joking when he claimed that his job had become so simple that all he had to do was hand the ball to Terrell Davis. Nonetheless, in the win over Cincinnati, Davis had rushed for at least 100 yards for the seventh consecutive game. And he was in the midst of the best season of his career; one in which he would rush for 2,008 yards and earn NFL MVP honors. With Denver's strong running game, Elway could often pick apart defenses because they were focused on stopping the run.

After the win over the Bengals, the Broncos returned home and easily dispatched the San Diego Chargers, 27-10. They then made their second Monday Night Football appearance of the season at Kansas City, where they squared off against the Chiefs. Early in Elway's career, the Broncos would probably have claimed that the Cleveland Browns were their fiercest rival, but the Chiefs had replaced them in the 1990s, when former Browns coach Marty Schottenheimer took over in Kansas City. Just a year before, the Broncos had lost a painfully close game to the Chiefs on Monday Night Football; now they turned things around with a blistering 30-7 victory. The Broncos were now 10–0 and the best team in the league! Pressure began to build, both in the locker room and from the media, as pundits, journalists, and fans alike wondered how long the Broncos could keep it up. Could they possibly equal the 1972 Miami Dolphins' record of going through the regular season without a loss?

In Week 12, Denver entertained the Oakland Raiders and gave them a 40-14 thrashing, as Elway threw three touchdown passes and joined Dan Marino as the only NFL quarterbacks to throw for 50,000 yards in their career. After an easy 31-16 win over the Chargers, the Broncos geared up for a rematch with the Chiefs on December 6. Again, the Broncos found themselves behind in the fourth quarter, as the Chiefs led, 31-21, with 8:25 left in the game. After Elway completed a 50-yard strike to wide receiver Willie Green to set up a Terrell Davis touchdown run, the Broncos' defense forced a three-and-out, giving Elway another shot at glory. Just five plays later, Elway had connected with tight end Shannon Sharpe on a 24-yard touchdown strike that put Denver ahead for good, 35-31. Elway passed for 400 yards that day, one of the best performances of his career, and the Broncos were suddenly 13–0 and had won 18 straight, dating back to the 1997 season. Up to this point, only two teams in NFL history (the 1934 Chicago Bears and the 1972 Miami Dolphins) had ever started the season 13–0.

MONDAY NIGHT FOOTBALL

No one expected Monday Night Football to become such a sensation, but almost from the very start it captured the imagination and interest of football fans, many of whom actually preferred the excitement of a Monday night shoot-out to Sunday afternoon games. The first Monday Night Football game aired on ABC on September 21, 1970, with the Cleveland Browns taking on the New York Jets. The Browns defeated the Jets, 31-21, as approximately a third of the country's television viewers tuned in. The first play-by-play announcer was Keith Jackson, with the color commentary supplied by Howard Cosell and Don Meredith. Cosell was best known for his work as a commentator for professional boxing, but what drew audiences to him was his outspokenness. Meredith was a former Dallas Cowboys quarterback who was known for his lighthearted and laid-back approach. In 1971, Jackson left to cover college football, and he was replaced by Frank Gifford, a former New York Giants quarterback and NFL announcer for CBS during the 1960s. The Gifford-Cosell-Meredith team carried Monday Night Football through most of the 1970s (although Meredith worked for rival NBC from 1974 to 1976 before returning in 1977).

Some Denver players declared that the pressure was becoming difficult to deal with, and a few even celebrated when they finally dropped a game, to the New York Giants, 20-16, on December 13. For many players, the unbeaten streak had become a burden, rather than a positive experience. There were just two games left in the regular season, and one of them was

Of the 20 most memorable Monday Night Football games—as selected by the editors of the *ESPN Pro Football Encyclopedia*—only one involved the Denver Broncos. This took place on October 17, 1994, when the Broncos and the Kansas City Chiefs squared off, with John Elway leading Denver and Joe Montana—in the twilight of his career—leading the Chiefs. The game was a classic matchup, but the two great quarterbacks saved their best for the last quarter. After the Chiefs took a 24-21 lead with about four minutes left in the game, Elway and the Broncos were set to work a little fourth-quarter magic. Unfortunately, tight end Shannon Sharpe fumbled the ball on the drive and the game seemed as if it might be over. However, Chiefs running back Marcus Allen fumbled the ball right back to the Broncos at their 39-yard line. A few plays later, Elway scored a touchdown on a third-and-goal from the Chiefs' 4-yard line. But Montana and the Chiefs still had 1:22 to work with. The Hall of Fame quarterback calmly marched his team down the field on a nine-play, 75-yard drive. With just 13 seconds left, Montana completed a five-yard touchdown strike to give the Chiefs a 31-28 win. Through the 2007 season, Denver had appeared on Monday Night Football a total of 55 times, with a 24–31 record.

considered a matchup between the "great ones": John Elway and Dan Marino.

Although they were both members of the 1983 NFL draft class, and though each had gone on to remarkable success, Elway and Marino had faced each other exactly once during their careers, back in 1985, when Miami had prevailed, 30-26. At this point, both players were at the end of their careers, and it was doubtful they would meet on the gridiron again, so both aging quarterbacks would attempt to pull out all their tricks for the Monday Night Football showdown. Elway had one of his poorer performances of the season, completing just 13 of 36 passes for 151 yards and two interceptions. On the other hand, Marino had a sizzling performance, completing 23 of 38 passes for 355 yards and four touchdowns as the Dolphins won, 31-21, dropping Denver's record to 13-2.

What Dan Marino and the Miami Dolphins did not know was that Mike Shanahan believed that it was more important to beat Miami in the playoffs, and he coached that way in the game. In *Think Like a Champion*, he stated:

> All I wanted to see was how the Dolphins aligned against various formations, how they matched up against our players and how they would defend [against] us. I used the Monday night game as a preview, a coming attraction, a major form of preparing. Now, would I tell our team that? No, of course I wouldn't.

In the Broncos' remaining regular-season contest, they beat Seattle, 28-21, as Elway completed 26 of 36 passes for 338 yards and four touchdowns. The win gave Denver a record of 14–2, the best in the franchise's 39-year history.

THE FINAL GO-AROUND

With their 14–2 record, the Broncos clinched the top seed in the AFC and home-field advantage throughout the playoffs.

John Elway celebrates as running back Terrell Davis scores his second touchdown of the day in the Broncos' 38-3 victory over Miami in the divisional round of the AFC playoffs on January 9, 1999. That season's league MVP, Davis rushed for 199 yards on 21 carries in the win over the Dolphins.

Meanwhile, the Dolphins were the fourth seed and had to play in the wild-card round of the playoffs. Behind 235 yards passing from Marino, the Dolphins beat the Buffalo Bills, 24-17, to set up a showdown at Mile High Stadium. Since the loss to the Dolphins, Coach Shanahan had been looking forward to a rematch with Miami in the playoffs. After the Dolphins' win over the Bills, Shanahan would get his wish. In *Think Like a Champion*, he recounted what happened during the game:

> The unbalanced line helped us control Miami middle linebacker Zach Thomas and create some big holes for Terrell Davis, who rushed for 199 yards on 21 carries in just over three quarters worth of work. The Dolphins hadn't even practiced against the formations we prepared for them. They were yelling at each other, knowing they were playing a more prepared Denver team than the one they beat up on down in Miami less than a month ago.

Sure enough, Denver walked away with an easy 38-3 win in the divisional round of the playoffs. Next, the Broncos would face the upstart New York Jets with the winner advancing to the Super Bowl.

On a windy, but fairly warm day in Denver, the story of the first half was **turnovers**. Each team had several opportunities to score, but only the Jets could muster points, taking a 3-0 lead into halftime. Then, early in the second half, disaster struck for the Broncos. Tom Rouen's punt was blocked by Jets tight end Blake Spence, who recovered the football on the 1-yard line. On the next play, Jets running back Curtis Martin scored to make it 10-0. But then the Broncos woke up. In just three plays, Elway directed the Broncos down the field and hit fullback Howard Griffith on an 11-yard touchdown pass that made it 10-7. The touchdown opened the floodgates, and the Broncos scored 23 unanswered points to win, 23-10, and advance to their second consecutive Super Bowl.

SUPER BOWL XXXIII

John Elway had appeared in four previous Super Bowls, winning one and losing three. As a franchise, the Denver Broncos had appeared in a total of five Super Bowls, winning just one. Now, for the first time in franchise history, the Broncos went into the Super Bowl as a prohibitive favorite to win. Their opponent was the Atlanta Falcons, coached by none other than Dan Reeves.

Since being fired as head coach of the Broncos after the 1992 season, Reeves had coached the New York Giants for four seasons and then, in 1997, moved on to Atlanta, where he transformed a mediocre team into the NFC's best in just two seasons. Not only had the Falcons posted the most wins in franchise history with their 14–2 regular-season record, but they were also making their first appearance in the Super Bowl. As for Coach Reeves, he was the same old Dan, charming and infuriating by turns, a man with a terrific mind but rather poor communication skills. But he had done something many considered impossible, taking the Falcons all the way to the Super Bowl, and now he was about to face two old friends and foes: John Elway and Mike Shanahan.

About 10 days before the Super Bowl, Reeves made some comments to the press about Shanahan and Elway. He brought up his old charge that they had tried to undermine him when Shanahan was quarterbacks coach in the early 1990s. He said: "If John Elway had a problem with me and you're coaching a position [such as Shanahan], why did I not know about that prior to reading it in the paper?" Reeves then reminded reporters that he had fired Shanahan in January 1992 for insubordination.

Elway and Shanahan were measured in their own responses, but they were privately delighted Reeves had made such a spectacle of himself, bringing up old wounds at a time when he should have been focusing all of his energies on the upcoming game. Within a few days, Reeves publicly apologized for bringing the matter up, but he had stepped into a messy situation: Reporters continued to ask him questions about the situation at every subsequent press conference.

For his part, Elway offered his comparison of his two NFL coaches to the *New York Times*—Dan Reeves, who had coached him between 1983 and 1992, and Shanahan, who had coached him from 1995 to 1999. "I do [believe Shanahan is better] and I think everyone knows the numbers back that up. I'm playing much better the last six years than I did the previous ten." And Coach Shanahan had this to say about Coach Reeves in *Think Like a Champion*:

> This was the last thing I was expecting. But at the NFL owners meetings in Phoenix in March 1999, who should walk right up to me, smiling, talking, acting like he's my best friend? None other than Dan Reeves, my former boss in Denver and the current Atlanta Falcons head coach. Dan comes right over to me as if he didn't criticize me two months earlier, didn't fire me eight years earlier, didn't charge me with insubordination. . . . He shakes my hand and acts like there had never been a single problem between us.

What Shanahan did not take into account was that Reeves had gone through major heart surgery one year earlier, an operation that changed his attitude toward many things. Reeves loved the game so much he had returned to coaching just three weeks after the surgery. But he did make some mistakes heading into Super Bowl XXXIII. A public relations war was carried out through the media, with Reeves claiming that Elway and Shanahan had conspired behind his back long ago, that they had scripted their own plays back when Shanahan was quarterbacks coach for Denver. Shanahan and Elway both fired back, and some observers were ready to call Super Bowl XXXIII the Bowl of Words. But the testy exchanges between the former friends and colleagues were supplanted by the actions of Falcons safety Eugene Robinson. On the same day he received the Bart Starr Award, presented annually to the

NFL player who best exemplifies outstanding character and leadership in the home, on the field, and in the community, Robinson got into some major trouble. The night before the Super Bowl, Robinson was arrested for soliciting a female undercover cop who was posing as a prostitute on Miami's Biscayne Boulevard. He spent a couple of hours in jail the night before the Super Bowl.

This was the same Eugene Robinson who had taunted the Denver Broncos during Super Bowl XXXII (of course, he had played for the Green Bay Packers at the time). Broncos players were ready for Robinson and his big mouth, as the moments ticked down to the game's start on January 31, 1999.

The Atlanta Falcons had a stronger running than passing game, and tailback Jamal Anderson started off fast, helping the Falcons get the ball all the way down to the Denver 8-yard line. Luckily, the Broncos' defense stepped up at just the right moment to force the Falcons to settle for a 32-yard Morten Andersen field goal, putting Atlanta up, 3-0. On the other side of the ball, the Broncos also wanted to establish the run. However, Elway handed the ball to Terrell Davis three times on their first drive and the sensational running back gained a grand total of four yards. Luckily, Elway then took to the air and connected with Rod Smith for a 41-yard gain. From there, he completed two passes to tight end Shannon Sharpe for 26 yards to get the Broncos down to the Atlanta 1-yard line. Then, fullback Howard Griffith, who had carried the ball a total of four times the entire season, lunged into the end zone to give Denver a 7-3 lead.

Denver soon had the ball again, but Elway was picked off as he tried to fire a pass from the shotgun formation, and the first quarter ended with Atlanta holding the ball in Denver territory. When the second quarter started, Coach Reeves took a big gamble, running the ball on fourth-and-inches. Denver stopped Anderson for a two-yard loss, and the Broncos took over on downs. Elway then led his team right down the field,

John Elway points to the Lombardi Trophy after helping the Broncos defeat the Atlanta Falcons, 34-19, in Super Bowl XXXIII. In Denver's second Super Bowl victory in as many years, Elway completed 18 of 29 passes for 336 yards and a touchdown on his way to being named MVP of the game.

but the Broncos had to settle for a 26-yard Jason Elam field goal rather than a touchdown, making the score 10-3 in Denver's favor. Atlanta responded, driving to the Denver 8-yard line, but

Andersen's 26-yard field-goal attempt missed wide right and the air seemed to go out of the Falcons. It was as if they had come further than they expected, and as if they were running out of gas at just the wrong moment.

Getting the ball once more, Elway dropped back, spotted an open target, and threw a magnificent pass to Rod Smith, who beat Eugene Robinson on the play, and then cruised all the way for an 80-yard touchdown. Suddenly the score was 17-3. The Falcons cut the lead to 17-6 on a 28-yard Andersen field goal, but things did not look good for them as they headed into halftime.

Both teams played well in the third quarter, but neither was able to score. After Broncos kicker Jason Elam missed a 38-yard field goal, quarterback Chris Chandler drove the Falcons to the Denver 41-yard line, but then threw the first of two third-quarter interceptions, as cornerback Darrius Johnson returned the ball to the Atlanta 42-yard line. Shortly thereafter, Elam missed another field goal, this time from 47 yards. The Falcons then reached the Denver 26-yard line, but Chandler threw a pass that was deflected and then intercepted by cornerback Darrien Gordon, who returned the ball all the way to the Atlanta 24-yard line. After a few plays, the third quarter ended with Denver standing at Atlanta's 1-yard line. As the fourth quarter began, Howard Griffith charged in for his second touchdown of the day, giving Denver a 24-6 lead.

Now trailing by three scores, the Falcons had little hope of coming back because their offense was based on the run, not the pass. On the next Falcons drive, Chandler was intercepted yet again by Gordon deep in Broncos territory, and the cornerback returned the ball to the Falcons' 48-yard line. On the next play, Elway hit Terrell Davis for a short pass, but the Broncos running back motored for 39 yards. A couple of plays later, Elway ran for a three-yard touchdown to give the Broncos a 31-6 lead. The Falcons were down, but not quite out. On the sidelines, backup Falcons quarterback Steve DeBerg (the same

(continues on page 116)

THE COMEBACK KID

During his 16-year NFL career, John Elway led the Denver Broncos to an NFL-record 47 fourth-quarter comebacks. Although Elway's most famous comeback win was during the 1986 AFC Championship Game—the 15-play, 98-yard drive that stuck a dagger in the hearts of Cleveland Browns fans—the Hall of Fame quarterback has led five other game-winning drives in postseason play, including one in Super Bowl XXXII. What follows is a list of Elway-led Denver fourth-quarter comebacks:

DATE	SCORE	DEFICIT
Dec. 11, 1983	DENVER 21, Baltimore 19	-19
Nov. 4, 1984	DENVER 26, New England 19	Tie
Nov. 11, 1984	Denver 16, SAN DIEGO 13	Tie
Dec. 9, 1984	DENVER 16, San Diego 13	Tie
Sept. 22, 1985	DENVER 44, Atlanta 28	-1
Nov. 11, 1985	DENVER 17, San Francisco 16	-6
Nov. 17, 1985	DENVER 30, San Diego 24 (OT)	-7
Dec. 1, 1985	Denver 31, PITTSBURGH 23	-6
Dec. 14, 1985	DENVER 14, Kansas City 13	-6
Dec. 20, 1985	Denver 27, SEATTLE 24	-7
Sept. 7, 1986	DENVER 38, L.A. Raiders 36	-5
Jan. 11, 1987*	Denver 23, CLEVELAND 20 (OT)	-7
Sept. 20, 1987	Denver 17, GREEN BAY 17 (OT)	-7
Nov. 16, 1987	DENVER 31, Chicago 29	-5
Dec. 6, 1987	DENVER 31, New England 20	-3
Jan. 17, 1988*	DENVER 38, Cleveland 33	Tie
Oct. 9, 1988	Denver 16, SAN FRANCISCO 13 (OT)	-7
Oct. 8, 1989	DENVER 16, San Diego 10	-1
Oct. 22, 1989	Denver 24, SEATTLE 21 (OT)	-7
Nov. 12, 1989	Denver 16, KANSAS CITY 13	Tie

Jan. 7, 1990*	DENVER 24, Pittsburgh 23	-6
Sept. 17, 1990	DENVER 24, Kansas City 23	-2
Oct. 21, 1990	Denver 27, INDIANAPOLIS 17	Tie
Oct. 20, 1991	DENVER 19, Kansas City 16	Tie
Oct. 27, 1991	Denver 9, NEW ENGLAND 6	Tie
Dec. 8, 1991	Denver 17, CLEVELAND 7	Tie
Dec. 15, 1991	DENVER 24, Phoenix 19	-2
Jan. 4, 1992*	DENVER 26, Houston 24	-1
Sept. 6, 1992	DENVER 17, L.A. Raiders 13	-3
Oct. 4, 1992	DENVER 20, Kansas City 19	-13
Oct. 18, 1992	DENVER 27, Houston 21	-1
Dec. 12, 1993	DENVER 27, Kansas City 21	-1
Oct. 23, 1994	Denver 20, SAN DIEGO 15	-1
Nov. 20, 1994	DENVER 32, Atlanta 28	-10
Sept. 17, 1995	DENVER 38, Washington 31	Tie
Nov. 19, 1995	DENVER 30, San Diego 27	Tie
Dec. 24, 1995	Denver 31, OAKLAND 28	-11
Sept. 15, 1996	DENVER 27, Tampa Bay 23	-3
Oct. 20, 1996	DENVER 45, Baltimore 34	-3
Nov. 4, 1996	Denver 22, OAKLAND 21	-5
Nov. 24, 1996	Denver 21, MINNESOTA 17	-3
Oct. 26, 1997	Denver 23, BUFFALO 20 (OT)	Tie
Nov. 2, 1997	DENVER 30, Seattle 27	Tie
Jan. 4, 1998*	Denver 14, KANSAS CITY 10	-3
Jan. 25, 1998+	Denver 31, Green Bay 24	Tie
Nov. 1, 1998	Denver 33, CINCINNATI 26	-5
Dec. 6, 1998	DENVER 35, Kansas City 31	-10

Home team in caps

* Playoff Game

+ Super Bowl

(continued from page 113)

DeBerg whom Elway had succeeded in Denver back in 1983) exhorted his teammates to keep the faith. The irony could not have been lost on anyone.

The Falcons had one last burst of energy, with Tim Dwight returning a kickoff 91 yards for a touchdown to make the score 31-13. After the Broncos recovered an onside kick attempt by the Falcons, they tacked on another field goal to make it 34-13 with about seven minutes left in the game. The Falcons scored one more touchdown with about two minutes left in the game but missed the two-point conversion, which made the final score 34-19. There would be no need for a comeback drive this time; with the win, Denver had become the sixth franchise to repeat as Super Bowl champions.

As sweet as the Super Bowl victory had been for Elway the year before, this win was even sweeter because he had a fantastic game. This time, in Super Bowl XXXIII, he completed 18 of 29 passes for 336 yards—the third-highest passing total in Super Bowl history. He also became the oldest player to score a touchdown in the Super Bowl, and his 80-yard touchdown strike to Rod Smith was the second-longest touchdown pass in Super Bowl history. Unanimously voted Super Bowl MVP, Elway basked in the glory of his second world championship. He had reached the pinnacle of the sport, at the advanced age of 38.

Owner Pat Bowlen held the Lombardi Trophy high in the air and shouted: "This one's for you!" Whether he meant the Denver fans, the Denver franchise, or all the millions of people who had rooted for the Broncos to repeat as world champions was uncertain.

Into the Sunset

Residents of the Mile High City partied as thoroughly as they had the previous year. The Broncos were on top of the world. Owner Pat Bowlen could not have been happier. Not only did the wins in Super Bowl XXXII and XXXIII vindicate the long struggle endured by Elway and his teammates, but the enthusiasm engendered by their victories ensured that Colorado voters would cast their ballots in support of a new stadium. (The last Broncos game at Mile High Stadium was played in 2000, and INVESCO Field at Mile High was completed in 2001).

STAY OR GO?

As for John Elway, he had broadly hinted, throughout 1998, that that season might be his last. Who could blame him if he chose this moment to retire, while he was on top of the game? As was usually the case, Elway turned to his father, Jack, for advice. The two sat up very late one night in April 1999, assessing the pros and cons of leaving the game he loved. If Elway returned, he might be able to ride the wave to another Super Bowl win, making it three in a row, which would surely put him in the record books. But father and son both knew the odds against a two-time championship team making it three in a row. History had shown that, in the free-agent era, it had become increasingly difficult to keep a great team together and earn the title of dynasty. Brett Favre had wowed everyone back in 1997, but he had not won a Super Bowl since. The Dallas Cowboys had been superb in the early 1990s, but they had taken a step back in the past couple of years.

Then there was the issue of injuries. Elway had had several surgeries during his career, playing through pain on many an occasion. He was one of the best in football at doing that, but the older he got, the more difficult it had become to recover from his injuries. Consequently, sometime after midnight, Jack and John Elway made their decision. This was it. John had played his last NFL game. He called Broncos owner Pat Bowlen, who was in Australia at the time, to tell him the news, then prepared to hold a press conference. But, as so often happens in life, something else intruded.

ANNOUNCING HIS RETIREMENT

Just about two days later, on April 20, something terrible happened 12 miles south of Denver at Columbine High School, in Littleton, Colorado. There was a horrendous shooting spree carried out by two disgruntled students, who killed 13 of their classmates and one teacher and injured 23 others. The perpetrators then turned their guns on themselves. Elway had planned to announce his retirement on April 21, but, out of respect for the families who were affected by the tragedy, he put off his announcement for another 10 days.

An emotional John Elway announces his retirement at a press conference at Broncos headquarters on May 2, 1999. During his 16-year NFL career, Elway established franchise records for passing yards (51,475) and touchdowns (300), was a nine-time Pro Bowl selection, and led the Broncos to their only two Super Bowl wins in franchise history.

So it was on Monday, May 2, 1999, that the Denver Broncos called a press conference to announce that John Elway planned to retire. There was hardly a dry eye in the place as Elway explained that all people move through stages in life. "We all graduate from high school," he pointed out, and we all keep graduating from other experiences, he said. "I'm just graduating from professional football." For the past 16 years, Elway had symbolized the Denver Broncos, embodying their long and painful struggle as a franchise to become the best team in the NFL. Now he was leaving.

Elway's career statistics, compiled during 16 years with the Broncos, were outstanding. Between 1983 and 1998, he

- Played in 234 games
- Rushed 774 times, for a total of 3,407 yards
- Attempted 7,250 passes, with 4,123 completions, for a 56.9 completion percentage
- Passed for a total of 51,475 yards, making him third best in NFL history at that point (behind Dan Marino and Fran Tarkenton)
- Passed for a total of 300 touchdowns
- Led his team to 47 fourth-quarter comebacks; the most in NFL history
- Won 148 games during his career

MOST WINS BY A QUARTERBACK IN NFL HISTORY

PLAYER	WINS	TEAM(S)
Brett Favre*	160	Green Bay
John Elway	148	Denver
Dan Marino	147	Miami
Fran Tarkenton	125	Minnesota, New York Giants
* Still active		

Critics—and there are always some—point out that Elway's numbers could have been even better, and focus on his 226 interceptions and 516 sacks as demerits against his overall performance. But anyone who watched Elway play, Sunday after Sunday, at times when his team's fate rested squarely on his shoulders and arm, recognized his talent and drive. He was a quarterback for the ages.

PERSONAL CHALLENGES AND LIFE BEYOND FOOTBALL

When he retired, Elway was just short of his thirty-ninth birthday, so he had many good years left. The question, however, was—what should he do? He had sold his five Denver area auto dealerships in 1997 for approximately $83 million. He could turn to politics (the Republican Party in Colorado hoped he would), but there seemed to be no way to improve on what he had already accomplished. An answer came in June 2002, when Elway became part owner and chief executive officer of the Colorado Crush, an Arena Football League team based in Denver. In his position with the Crush, Elway is primarily responsible for day-to-day football operations, including player personnel decisions. Under Elway's leadership, the Crush won the 2005 AFL title, defeating the Georgia Force, 51-48. More recently, in February 2007, Elway was named chairman of the AFL's executive committee, which works closely with the AFL commissioner to shape league policy. The AFL has been a positive experience for Elway: "It's been a chance for me to stay close to football. . . . It's replaced a little bit of what I lost when I retired from the NFL," Elway said of his involvement with the Crush. "You can never replace it entirely but you're always looking for something that comes close to it."

Outside of football, Elway has given a lot back to the community. He has his own nonprofit organization, the Elway Foundation, which he and his former wife, Janet, established in 1987. The foundation works primarily with the Kempe Children's Foundation and Family Advocacy Care Education and Support

(F.A.C.E.S.), each of which helps to prevent and treat child abuse. Elway's foundation has raised more than $6 million for this cause, including more than $3 million through the annual Elway

THE CLASS OF 1983

Back in 1983, when John Elway was selected as the number-one overall pick by the Baltimore Colts, there were a number of other very promising quarterbacks who were also drafted that year. Often referred to as the Quarterback Class of 1983, that year's draft set an NFL record with six quarterbacks chosen in the first round. So how did the others fare in their NFL careers?

The last of the six to be drafted was Dan Marino, who was the twenty-seventh overall pick. However, Marino may have had the best NFL career. Some of his numbers were better than Elway's. Never the great rusher that Elway was, Marino set several NFL records, including pass attempts (8,358), completions (4,967), passing yards (61,361), and touchdown passes (420). Although Green Bay Packers quarterback Brett Favre has since broken all of these records, some consider Marino the greatest quarterback of all time. Unfortunately, the 2005 NFL Hall of Fame inductee never won a Super Bowl (he and the Dolphins lost Super Bowl XIX to the San Francisco 49ers, 38-16).

Like Elway and Marino, Jim Kelly played his entire NFL career with one franchise—the Buffalo Bills. The fourteenth overall pick in the 1983 draft, Kelly first played in the USFL for two years with the Houston Gamblers. When that league folded after the 1985 season, he joined the Bills. In 11 seasons with the Bills, he helped lead the team to four straight Super Bowls; unfortunately, Buffalo lost each one. But Kelly's career statistics were impressive by any standard. In just 160 games, he completed 2,874 of 4,779 passes for 35,467 yards and 237

Golf Classic, a celebrity golf tournament held each summer in Denver. For his charitable work, Elway was named the Walter Payton NFL Man of the Year recipient in 1992.

touchdowns. He was a five-time Pro Bowler and still holds the NFL record for most yards gained per completion in a game (44) and the Super Bowl record for pass attempts in a game (58). He was inducted into the Pro Football Hall of Fame in 2002.

The other three quarterbacks in the class did not have Hall of Fame careers, but two of the three started for several years in the NFL. The twenty-fourth overall pick in the draft by the New York Jets, Ken O'Brien was the primary starter for the Jets for nine seasons. He was a two-time Pro Bowler and threw for 25,094 yards and 128 touchdowns during his career. The fifteenth overall pick in the draft by the Patriots, Tony Eason played eight years in the NFL, mostly with New England, where he was the primary starter for three seasons. In his career, he threw for 11,142 yards and 61 touchdowns. Finally, Todd Blackledge was the seventh overall pick in the draft by the Kansas City Chiefs. He was the primary starter for the Chiefs for three seasons and played a total of seven seasons in the NFL, moving from Kansas City to Pittsburgh in 1988. He passed for just 5,286 yards and 29 touchdowns in a disappointing career.

So who came out as "the best"? On any given day, Jim Kelly could outthrow Dan Marino who could, in turn, outthrow John Elway, and the reverse was equally true. But in terms of individual performance meeting team performance, one would have to say that Elway's fine statistics, along with his two Super Bowl rings, puts him on top of the "Class of 1983."

Elway has indeed kept himself busy since he retired in 1999, but he also has been forced to deal with a number of personal challenges. His wife, Janet, had part of her colon removed in August 1998. The operation was to remove the threat of cancer, but she got an infection while in the hospital, and though she recovered well, she still feels fatigued from time to time.

Elway's father, Jack, died of a heart attack in April 2001, at the age of 69. Those who knew how close John and Jack had always been were sure that John would find it difficult not to have his father around. For the first time in his life, his father was not there to look out for him and give him advice.

Then, in June 2002, John and Janet separated. There had long been rumors that the marriage was strained, and the separation confirmed many of them. There was no lack of love between John and Janet Elway, but football had always come first, and it was difficult for Janet to accept. After they split up, she told the *Rocky Mountain News*: "I used to feel like I had to share my husband with the rest of the world, and I wanted him to just be mine, and I couldn't ever really ask that." Remarkably, just when Elway's football career had ended, his marriage was falling apart.

Jana Elway, John's twin sister, died of cancer in August 2002. Coming on the heels of his father's death and his marital troubles, this new shock brought Elway to a new low. To demonstrate her loyalty to her husband, Janet reconciled with John and the two lived together for a few months, but in January 2003, he confirmed to the press that the couple had separated and were seeking a divorce.

Could anything more go wrong?

Elway's own health remained excellent, as it had throughout most of his life, but he had plenty of old sports injuries from which to recover. His finances were in good shape. Not only had he made plenty of money during his years in the NFL, but, as mentioned, he made money from the sale of his automobile dealerships in 1997. He was also doing well in the Arena Football League, and he had a number of endorsement deals with various businesses. At one time, there was speculation he might become a part owner of the Broncos franchise, but this did not come to fruition.

THE CARTOON ELWAY

John Elway arrived in Denver in 1983, triggering "Elway Fever." At about the same time, a young cartoonist with the *Rocky Mountain News* made Elway into one of his favorite characters, leading to a series of Elway cartoons that chronicled the Hall of Fame quarterback's career from the days of Dan Reeves to Elway's induction into the Pro Football Hall of Fame.

Drew Litton described Elway as a perfect stooge for a willing cartoonist. The toothy smile, long hair, and "aw-shucks" manner were perfect fodder for newspaper cartoons. Some of the funniest had to do with Marty Schottenheimer, head coach of the Cleveland Browns and then the Kansas City Chiefs. Elway beat Schottenheimer's teams in innumerable encounters, and one cartoon showed Schottenheimer shaving "The Morning After" and finding John Elway doing a "nah-nah-I-got-you" type of pose in the mirror. Another cartoon lampooned Elway's distaste for cold weather (he had always been a warm-weather player at heart), showing the great player shivering in a chair, wrapped in an electric blanket while his mother told his teammates, "I'm sorry but Johnny can't come out and play in the snow, his little hands might get cold."

Elway took the ribbing well. He had always enjoyed a good laugh, whether at the situation or at himself. He may well have been pleased when Litton's many cartoons were bundled together in the book *Give My Regards to Elway: A Cartoon Tribute to John Elway*, which was published right before Elway was inducted into the Pro Football Hall of Fame in 2004.

On August 8, 2004, Elway was inducted into the Pro Football Hall of Fame, winning admittance on the first ballot. He gave a gracious acceptance speech, though critics pointed out he had not mentioned his former wife. As he surveyed the situation in 2004, Elway had plenty of reason to be content. Even though there were a few up-and-coming quarterbacks in the league, none had yet equaled him, with the possible exceptions of Brett Favre and Peyton Manning.

Favre, whom Elway had bested in the 1998 Super Bowl, had the most incredible statistic of all: He had started 253 consecutive games through the 2007 season; he had not missed a single game since 1992! Manning, whom Elway had never played against, was accumulating a long string of consecutive starts as well, and he was quickly becoming recognized as one of the great quarterbacks of all time. Like Elway, Manning had been criticized early in his career; some experts said he did fine during the regular season but could not win the big game. (Manning and the Indianapolis Colts lost several times in the playoffs.) But he put those doubts to rest by leading the Colts to a 29-17 victory over the Chicago Bears in Super Bowl XLI.

THE MAN AND THE LEGEND

No one knows—perhaps not even John Elway—who truly is the "best" quarterback of all time. There is no way to put great players such as Johnny Unitas (1950s and 1960s), Roger Staubach (1970s), Terry Bradshaw (1970s), and Joe Montana (1980s and 1990s) on an even playing field. They made the best plays they could during their careers, and took plenty of criticism, as well as accepting many congratulations.

No one knows what demons great champions face when they strive to be the best. They may have nightmares about games they lost, or they may be able to shrug off defeat and disappointment. However, Elway put it well in *Comeback Kid* when he said:

John Elway's oldest daughter, Jessica, stands next to her father after his induction ceremony into the Pro Football Hall of Fame, on August 8, 2004, in Canton, Ohio. Jessica was the first player's daughter to present her father for induction into the Hall of Fame.

The thing I've noticed about people who are winners is that, to them, losing is always temporary. The great thing about playing sports—and about life—is you can always redeem yourself in the next game or the next season. A winner is someone who is able to come back from defeat.

John Elway did that, many times.

STATISTICS

JOHN ELWAY
POSITION: Quarterback

FULL NAME: John Albert Elway
BORN: June 28, 1960,
Port Angeles, Washington
HEIGHT: 6'3"
WEIGHT: 215 lbs.

COLLEGE: Stanford
TEAM: Denver
Broncos (1983–1998)

YEAR	TEAM	G	COMP	ATT	PCT	YD	Y/A	TD	INT
1983	DEN	11	123	259	47.5	1,663	6.4	7	14
1984	DEN	15	214	380	56.3	2,598	6.8	18	15
1985	DEN	16	327	605	54.0	3,891	6.4	22	23
1986	DEN	16	280	504	55.6	3,485	6.9	19	13
1987	DEN	12	224	410	54.6	3,198	7.8	19	12
1988	DEN	15	274	496	55.2	3,309	6.7	17	19
1989	DEN	15	223	416	53.6	3,051	7.3	18	18
1990	DEN	16	294	502	58.6	3,526	7.0	15	14
1991	DEN	16	242	451	53.7	3,253	7.2	13	12
1992	DEN	12	174	316	55.1	2,242	7.1	10	17
1993	DEN	16	348	551	63.2	4,030	7.3	25	10
1994	DEN	14	307	494	62.1	3,490	7.1	16	10
1995	DEN	16	316	542	58.3	3,970	7.3	26	14
1996	DEN	15	287	466	61.6	3,328	7.1	26	14
1997	DEN	16	280	502	55.8	3,635	7.2	27	11
1998	DEN	13	210	356	59.0	2,806	7.9	22	10
TOTALS		234	4,123	7,250	56.9	51,475	7.1	300	226

CHRONOLOGY

1960 John Elway born in Port Angeles, Washington.

1961 The Elways move to Aberdeen, Washington, where Jack Elway serves as head football coach of Grays Harbor College until 1966.

1966 The family moves to Missoula, Montana, where Jack becomes an assistant coach at the University of Montana.

1971 Jack Elway becomes an assistant at his alma mater, Washington State, and the family moves to Pullman.

1976 The Elways move to southern California, where Jack becomes head coach at Cal State Northridge.

1978–1979 During his senior season at Granada Hills (Calif.) High School, Elway is selected by the Kansas City Royals in the eighteenth round of the Major League Baseball draft, but decides to attend Stanford University on a football scholarship.

1980 Named first-team All-American by *Sporting News*.

1982 Elway is drafted by the New York Yankees in 1981 and later plays baseball for their Class-A affiliate Oneonta, where he bats .318 with 25 RBI in 42 games; during his senior season at Stanford, the Cardinal finishes 5–6 and loses to rival Cal on the last play of the game, 25-20; Elway finishes as runner-up for the Heisman Trophy and is again named first-team All-American by *Sporting News*.

1983 **April** Elway is selected number one overall in the NFL draft by the Baltimore Colts, but refuses to sign with the team.

May Colts trade the rights to Elway to the Denver Broncos for quarterback Mark Herrmann, offensive lineman Chris Hinton, and a first-round pick in the 1984 draft; Elway signs a six-year, $12.7 million contract with the Broncos.

September 4 Elway makes his debut for the Broncos against Pittsburgh but completes just 1 of 8 passes for 14 yards and is sacked four times.

October 9 Elway is replaced at quarterback by Steve DeBerg and sits the next four games.

December 11 In the best performance of his rookie season, Elway completes 23 of 44 passes for 345 yards and three touchdowns to rally the Broncos from a 9-0 deficit and take a 21-19 win over the Baltimore Colts.

1984 Elway marries Janet Buchan in California, and the couple settles in Denver; Elway leads the Broncos to a 13–3 regular-season record, as he throws for 2,598

TIMELINE

1960
Born in Port Angeles, Washington

1982
Plays minor league baseball for New York Yankees; runner-up for Heisman Trophy

1985
Sets single-season-Broncos records for attempts, completions, passing yards, and total offense

1960 ——— **1987**

1979
Enrolls at Stanford University, where he plays football and baseball

1983
Selected number-one in NFL draft by Baltimore

1987
Leads Broncos on "The Drive" to win AFC Championship

yards, but the team loses to the Pittsburgh Steelers in the first round of the playoffs.

1985   Elway sets single-season team records for attempts (605), completions (327), passing yards (3,891), and total offense (4,414 yards).

1986   Elway leads the Broncos to an 11–5 regular-season record after passing for 3,485 yards.

1987   **January 11** Elway executes "The Drive" against the Cleveland Browns in AFC Championship Game, leading the Broncos to a 23-20 win.
January 25 Despite completing 22 of 37 passes for 304 yards, Elway and the Broncos are beaten by the

1995
Mike Shanahan hired as Broncos head coach

1998
Broncos win first Super Bowl in franchise history, defeating the Green Bay Packers

2004
Inducted into the Pro Football Hall of Fame

1990

2004

1990
Leads Broncos to their third Super Bowl appearance in four years, but the team loses again

1997
Becomes just the second quarterback in NFL history to top the 50,000-yard mark in total offense

1999
Leads Broncos to their second consecutive Super Bowl victory, this time over the Atlanta Falcons

JOHN ELWAY

New York Giants in Super Bowl XXI, 39-20. During the 1987 regular season, Elway is named NFL MVP by the Associated Press after passing for 3,198 yards in a strike-shortened season (12 games).

1988   Elway again leads the Broncos to the Super Bowl, but this time they are routed by the Washington Redskins, 42-10.

1989   Elway leads the Broncos to an 11–5 regular-season record after passing for 3,051 yards.

1990   Elway leads the Broncos to their third Super Bowl appearance in four years after passing for 385 yards and three touchdowns in a 37-21 win against Cleveland in the AFC Championship Game; unfortunately, the Broncos suffer their worst defeat in team history, losing 55-10 to the San Francisco 49ers in Super Bowl XXIV, as Elway completes just 10 of 26 passes for 108 yards; during the 1990 regular season, Broncos post their worst record (5–11) since 1982, but Elway completes 58.6 percent of his passes (his highest rate during the first 10 years of his career) for 3,526 yards and 15 touchdowns.

1991   Elway considers asking to be traded; Broncos finish 12–4 and advance to the AFC Championship Game, where they lose to the Buffalo Bills, 10-7.

1992–1993   Dan Reeves is fired as Broncos head coach after the team finishes 8–8 in 1992; Broncos hire defensive coordinator Wade Phillips as head coach, and Denver finishes 9–7 in 1993; Elway throws for 4,030 yards, the only time during his 16-year career that he tops the 4,000-yard plateau.

1994   Denver loses to Oakland, 42-24, in the wild-card round of the playoffs; Broncos finish 7–9 during 1994 regular season, but Elway throws for 3,490 yards, topping the 3,000-yard mark for the ninth time in his career.

1995   Wade Phillips fired after just two years as Broncos head coach; he is replaced by San Francisco 49ers offensive coordinator Mike Shanahan, who previously served as an assistant with Denver; Broncos finish 8–8, as Elway establishes new career highs with 26 touchdown passes and five 300-yard passing games.

1996   Broncos win AFC West Division with a 13–3 regular season record, as Elway becomes only the third player in NFL history to pass for more than 45,000 yards.

1997   Broncos are upset in the divisional round of the AFC playoffs by the second-year Jacksonville Jaguars, 30-27; during the 1997 regular season, Elway leads the Broncos to a 12–4 regular-season record as he tosses a career-high 27 touchdown passes and becomes just the second quarterback in NFL history to top the 50,000-yard mark in total offense.

1998   Broncos get revenge in a 42-17 win over Jacksonville in the wild-card round of the playoffs in Denver; during the next two weeks, the Broncos go on the road and defeat Kansas City, 14-10, and Pittsburgh, 24-21, to advance to the Super Bowl; although Elway only completes 12 of 22 passes for 123 yards, the Broncos win the first Super Bowl in franchise history, defeating the Green Bay Packers, 31-24.

November 22 Elway joins Dan Marino as the only two players in NFL history to throw for 50,000 yards.

December 6 In a 35-31 win against Kansas City, Elway leads the Broncos to the 47th and final game-winning drive of his career.

December 27 In the final regular-season game of his career, Elway throws four touchdown passes in a 28-21 win against Seattle to reach 300 for his career; Denver finishes 14–2, as Elway records his NFL-record 148th career win.

1999   Elway leads the Broncos to playoff wins against Miami, 38-3, and the New York Jets, 23-10, to reach the fifth Super Bowl of his career; in Super Bowl XXXIII, the Broncos defeat the Atlanta Falcons, 34-19, as Elway completes 18 of 29 passes for 336 yards to earn MVP honors and go out on top.

May 2 Elway announces that he is retiring from the NFL.

September 13 Elway's number is retired by the Broncos.

2004   **August 8** Elway inducted into the Pro Football Hall of Fame.

GLOSSARY

All Pro   A designation, or honor, accorded to those who are selected to play in the NFL Pro Bowl, held at the end of each football season.

American Football Conference (AFC)   One of the two conferences in the National Football League (NFL). The AFC was established after the NFL merged with the American Football League (AFL) in 1970.

audible   A play called by the quarterback at the line of scrimmage to change the play that was called in the huddle.

backup   A second-string player who does not start the game, but comes in later in relief of a starter.

blitz   A defensive maneuver in which one or more linebackers or defensive backs, who normally remain behind the line of scrimmage, instead charge into the opponent's backfield.

blocking   When a player obstructs another player's path with his body. Examples: cut block, zone block, trap block, pull block, screen block, pass block, and double-team block.

bootleg   An offensive play predicated upon misdirection in which the quarterback pretends to hand the ball to another player and then carries the ball in the opposite direction of the supposed ballcarrier with the intent of either passing or running (sometimes the quarterback has the option of doing either).

center   A player position on offense. The center snaps the ball.

chain   The 10-yard-long chain that is used by the chain crew (aka, "chain gang") to measure for a new series of downs.

completion percentage   The percentage of passes thrown by a player that are completed. For example, if a running back throws one pass all season and completes it, his completion percentage would be 100 percent.

cornerback   A defensive back who lines up near the line of scrimmage across from a wide receiver. His primary job is to disrupt passing routes and to defend against short and medium passes in the passing game and to contain the rusher on running plays.

defensive back   A cornerback or safety position on the defensive team; commonly defends against wide receivers on passing plays. Generally there are four defensive backs playing at a time.

defensive end   A player position on defense who lines up on the outside of the defensive line whose principal function is to deliver pressure to the quarterback.

defensive tackle   A player position on defense on the inside of the defensive line whose principal function is to contain the run.

drive   A continuous set of offensive plays gaining substantial yardage and several first downs, usually leading to a scoring opportunity.

end zone   The area between the end line and the goal line, bounded by the sidelines.

extra point   A single point scored in a conversion attempt by place- or drop-kicking the ball through the opponent's goal.

field goal   Score of three points made by place- or drop-kicking the ball through the opponent's goal.

first down   The first of a set of four downs. Usually, a team that has a first down needs to advance the ball 10 yards to receive another first down, but penalties or field position (i.e., less than 10 yards from the opposing end zone) can affect this.

formation   An arrangement of the offensive skill players.

fourth down   The final of a set of four downs. Unless a first down is achieved or a penalty forces a replay of the down, the team will lose control of the ball after this play. If a team does not think they can get a first down, they often punt on fourth down or kick a field goal if they are close enough to do so.

fullback   A player position on offense. In modern formations, this position may be varied, and this player has more blocking responsibilities in comparison to the halfback or tailback.

fumble   A ball that a player accidentally loses possession of.

goal line   The front of the end zone.

guard   One of two player positions on offense (linemen).

handoff   A player's handing of a live ball to another player. The handoff goes either backwards or laterally, as opposed to a forward pass.

holding   There are two kinds of holding: offensive holding, illegally blocking a player from the opposing team by grabbing and holding his uniform or body; and defensive holding, called against defensive players who impede receivers who are more than five yards from the line of scrimmage, but who are not actively making an attempt to catch the ball.

huddle   An on-field gathering of members of a team in order to secretly communicate instructions for the upcoming play.

incomplete pass   A forward pass of the ball that no player legally caught.

interception   The legal catching of a forward pass thrown by an opposing player.

kickoff   A free kick that starts each half, or restarts the game following a touchdown or field goal.

line of scrimmage/scrimmage line   One of two vertical planes parallel to the goal line when the ball is to be put in play by scrimmage.

linebacker   A player position on defense. The linebackers typically play one to six yards behind the defensive linemen and are the most versatile players on the field because they can play both run and pass defense or are called to blitz.

man-to-man coverage   A defense in which all players in pass coverage, typically linebackers and defensive backs, cover a specific player.

National Collegiate Athletic Association (NCAA)   Principal governing body of college sports, including college football.

National Football Conference (NFC)   One of the two conferences in the National Football League (NFL). The NFC was established after the NFL merged with the American Football League (AFL) in 1970.

National Football League (NFL)   The largest professional American football league, with 32 teams.

offside   An infraction of the rule that requires both teams to be on their own side of their restraining line as or before the ball is put in play. Offside is typically called on the defensive team.

option   A type of play in which the quarterback has the option of handing off, keeping, or laterally passing to one or more backs. Often described by a type of formation or play action, such as triple option, veer option, or counter option.

pass interference   When a player illegally hinders an eligible receiver's opportunity to catch a forward pass.

passer rating   (*also* **quarterback rating**) A numeric value used to measure the performance of quarterbacks. It was formulated in 1973 and it uses the player's completion percentage, passing yards, touchdowns, and interceptions.

play action   A tactic in which the quarterback fakes either a handoff or a throw in order to draw the defense away from the intended offensive method.

pocket   An area on the offensive side of the line of scrimmage, where the offensive linemen attempt to prevent the defensive players from reaching the quarterback during passing plays.

position   A place where a player plays relative to teammates, and/or a role filled by that player.

punt   A kick in which the ball is dropped and kicked before it reaches the ground. Used to give up the ball to the opposition after offensive downs have been used.

quarterback   An offensive player who lines up behind the center, from whom he takes the snap.

reception   When a player catches (receives) the ball.

running back   A player position on offense. Although the term usually refers to the halfback or tailback, fullbacks are also considered running backs.

sack   Tackling a ballcarrier who intends to throw a forward pass. A sack is also awarded if a player forces a fumble of the ball, or the ballcarrier to go out of bounds, behind the line of scrimmage on an apparent intended forward pass play.

safety   A player position on defense; a method of scoring (worth two points) by downing an opposing ballcarrier in his own end zone, forcing the opposing ballcarrier out of his own end zone and out of bounds, or forcing the offensive team to fumble the ball so that it exits the end zone.

salary cap   A limit on the amount any NFL team can spend on its players' salaries; the salary cap was introduced in 1994 in order to bring parity to the NFL.

scramble   On a called passing play, when the quarterback runs from the pocket in an attempt to avoid being sacked, giving the receivers more time to get open or attempting to gain positive yards by running himself.

secondary   Refers to the defensive "backfield," specifically the safeties and cornerbacks.

shotgun formation   Formation in which the offensive team may line up at the start of a play. In this formation, the quarterback receives the snap five to eight yards behind the center.

sideline   One of the lines marking each side of the field.

snap　The handoff or pass from the center that begins a play from scrimmage.

special teams　The units that handle kickoffs, punts, free kicks, and field-goal attempts.

squib kick　A kickoff in football in which the ball bounces along the ground.

starter　A player who is the first to play his position within a given game or season. Depending on the position and the game situation, this player may be replaced or share time with one or more players later in the game. For example, a quarterback may start the game but be replaced by a backup quarterback if the game becomes one-sided.

tackle　The act of forcing a ballcarrier to the ground. Also, a position on the offensive and defensive line.

tailback　Player position on offense farthest ("deepest") back, except in kicking formations.

tight end　A player position on offense, often known as a Y receiver when he lines up on the line of scrimmage, next to the offensive tackle. Tight ends are used as blockers during running plays and either run a route or stay in to block during passing plays.

time of possession　The amount of time one team has the ball in its possession relative to the other team.

touchdown　A play worth six points, accomplished by gaining legal possession of the ball in the opponent's end zone. It also allows the team a chance for one extra point by kicking the ball or a chance to attempt a two-point conversion.

turnover　The loss of the ball by one team to the other team. This is usually the result of a fumble or an interception.

West Coast offense　An offensive philosophy that uses short, high-percentage passes as the core of a ball-control offense.

wide receiver　A player position on offense. He is split wide (usually about 10 yards) from the formation and plays on the line of scrimmage as a split end (X) or one yard off as a flanker (Z).

wild card   The two playoff spots given to the two nondivision-winning teams that have the best records in each conference.

wishbone   A formation involving three running backs lined up behind the quarterback in the shape of a Y, similar to the shape of a wishbone.

yard   One yard of linear distance in the direction of one of the two goals. A field is 100 yards. Typically, a team is required to advance at least 10 yards in order to get a new set of downs.

zone defense   A defense in which players who are in pass coverage cover zones of the field, instead of individual players.

BIBLIOGRAPHY

Callahan, Tom. "Two-Way Elway Gets His Way," *Time,* May 16, 1983, p. 69.

Elway, John, with Greg Brown. *Comeback Kid.* Dallas: Taylor Publishing, 1997.

Eskenazi, Gerald. "After Opening Wounds, Reeves Says He's Sorry," *New York Times,* January 25, 1999, p. D4.

Fimrite, Ron. "The Anatomy of a Miracle," *Sports Illustrated,* September 1, 1983, p. 218.

Gay, Timothy, Ph.D. *The Physics of Football.* New York: Harper Collins, 2005.

Giglio, Joe. *Great Teams in Pro Football History.* Chicago: Raintree, 2006.

Hirshberg, Dan. *John Elway.* Philadelphia: Chelsea House, 1997.

Jaworski, Ron, Pete Palmer, Ken Pullis, and Sean Lahman, eds. *The ESPN Pro Football Encyclopedia.* New York: Sterling Publishing, 2006.

Latimer, Clay. *John Elway: Armed and Dangerous.* Lenexa, Kans.: Addax Publishing, 1998.

Litton, Drew. *Give My Regards to Elway: A Cartoon Tribute to John Elway.* Boulder, Colo.: Johnson Books, 2000.

Lyon, Bill. *When the Clock Runs Out: 20 NFL Greats Share Their Stories of Hardship and Triumph.* Chicago: Triumph Books, 1999.

MacCambridge, Michael, ed. *ESPN College Football Encyclopedia: The Complete History of the Game.* New York: ESPN Books, 2006.

Shanahan, Mike, with Adam Schefter. *Think Like a Champion: Building Success One Victory at a Time.* New York: Harper Collins, 1999.

Stewart, Mark. *Terrell Davis: Toughing it Out.* Brookfield, Conn.: Millbrook Press, 1999.

Zimmer, Larry. *Stadium Stories: Denver Broncos*. Guilford, Conn.: Globe Pequot Press, 2004.

Zimmerman, Paul. "Super Star: The Giants' Phil Simms," cover story, *Sports Illustrated*, February 2, 1987, p. 24.

———. "One Super Show," cover story, *Sports Illustrated*, February 8, 1988, p. 26.

———. "Joe Knows Super Bowls," cover story, *Sports Illustrated*, February 5, 1990, p. 22.

FURTHER READING

Giglio, Joe. *Great Teams in Pro Football History*. Chicago: Raintree, 2006.

Hirshberg, Dan. *John Elway*. Philadelphia, Pa.: Chelsea House, 1997.

Latimer, Clay. *John Elway: Armed and Dangerous*. Lenexa, Kans.: Addax Publishing, 1998.

Litton, Drew. *Give My Regards to Elway: A Cartoon Tribute to John Elway*. Boulder, Colo.: Johnson Books, 2000.

Shanahan, Mike, with Adam Schefter. *Think Like a Champion: Building Success One Victory at a Time*. New York: Harper Collins, 1999.

WEB SITES

Denver Broncos Tribute Page to John Elway
http://www.denverbroncos.com/page.php?id=1055

John Elway's Official Web site
http://www.johnelway.com/

NFL.com: John Elway Player Profile
http://www.nfl.com/players/johnelway/profile?id=ELW276861

John Elway Scrapbook
http://www.sportingnews.com/archives/elway/

PICTURE CREDITS

COVER

AP Images

INDEX

ABOUT THE AUTHOR

One year younger than John Elway, SAMUEL WILLARD CROMPTON remembers the sports of the 1980s and 1990s well, even though he followed tennis more than football. He is a major contributor to the *American National Biography* (1999) and *Scribner's Encyclopedia of American Lives*—the two-volume sports edition. Crompton lives and works in the Berkshire Hills of his native western Massachusetts.